opposing viewpoints®

america's economy

1987 annual

David L. Bender, *Publisher*
Bruno Leone, *Executive Editor*
M. Teresa O'Neill, *Senior Editor*
Bonnie Szumski, *Senior Editor*
Janelle Rohr, *Senior Editor*
Lynn Hall, *Editor*
Susan Bursell, *Editor*
Julie S. Bach, *Editor*
Neal Bernards, *Editor*
Thomas Modl, *Editor*
Karin Swisher, *Editorial Assistant*

greenhaven press, inc.

577 Shoreview Park Road
St. Paul, MN 55126

ISBN 0-89908-531-8
ISSN 0889-4299

contents

Editor's Note   *Opposing Viewpoints SOURCES* provide a wealth of opinions on important issues of the day. The annual supplements focus on the topics that continue to generate debate. Readers will find that *Opposing Viewpoints SOURCES* become exciting barometers of today's controversies. This is achieved in three ways. First, by expanding previous chapter topics. Second, by adding new materials which are timeless in nature. And third, by adding recent topical issues not dealt with in previous volumes or annuals. Viewpoint numbers are consecutive from Vol. 1.

Viewpoints

"Creditors must accept a share of the sacrifices needed to resolve the Third World debt crisis."

Lender Nations Must Help End the World Debt Crisis

Rembert Weakland

Editor's note: Archbishop Rembert Weakland addressed the issue of the international debt problem before the US House subcommittee on foreign operations on behalf of the U.S. Catholic Conference. In November 1986, US Catholic bishops approved a pastoral letter on the US economy entitled, "Economic Justice for All."

One might think from accounts in the media that the so-called debt crisis burst full-blown and unexpectedly on the world in August 1982, when Mexico announced that it could not meet its debt-servicing requirements. In fact, however, as you know, it had been accumulating throughout the 1970s at least, as food and energy prices rose sharply and newly rich oil-exporting countries invested their profits in the banks of the industrialized countries. Developing countries borrowed these funds to pay their increased energy and other import bills—and then borrowed again when oil prices doubled once more at the end of the decade and falling prices for their commodity exports reduced their ability to service the debts incurred earlier.

The Brandt Commission

Already at the beginning of the 1980's, before commercial lending began to decline and nearly three years before the Mexican announcement, the Brandt Commission noted that the borrowing needs of even the better-off developing countries were likely to rise considerably during the ensuing decade, at least partly because they would need to borrow more in order to service the debt already accrued. The commission went on to observe that "the debtor economies and the entire international credit structure are now very vulnerable to any disruptions

in the flows of capital." "The heart of the debt problem," it said, "is that a very large proportion of the funds are lent on terms which are onerous for borrowers from the point of view of both the repayment capacity of the projects they finance and the time debtor countries need to correct structural imbalances in their external accounts."

What is not always recognized is that developing-country borrowing saved the industrialized countries from the full impact of the oil price rise. "Over the last few years," the commission continued, "economic activity in the industrialized countries has been sustained by a major recycling of financial surpluses through the commercial banks." The commission quoted an Organization for Economic Cooperation and Development report that says, "Had developing countries followed the example of industrialized countries after 1973, by cutting back both their growth and imports to adjust to the oil price increase, the recession in the industrialized world would have been far more serious."

In other words, these countries of the South bailed out the industrialized countries of the North by quadrupling their own external debt in the decade of the 1970s. When oil prices doubled again in 1979, they were unable to repeat that performance, especially during the recession that ensued and as the term of trade worsened for their exports. At the end of 1979 their debt was about $300 billion; the Brandt Commission estimated that another $500 billion might have to be added by 1985 unless the oil-importing countries checked their imports and their growth—"provided the funds could be found." As is manifest in the $1 trillion total, those funds were found until recently.

The Brandt Commission's prescription for relief was "massive transfers" of resources through concessional foreign aid and commercial lending, which would require "intermediation" by public institutions like the World Bank and the

Rembert Weakland, testimony before the US House Subcommittee on Foreign Operations on March 4, 1987.

International Monetary Fund, since "private commercial banks . . . can no longer be counted on to conduct the recycling process unassisted." "All countries must share the burden," the commission said and called for, among other things, a system of universal international taxation.

As we all know, all countries have not shared the burden; commercial lending has dwindled to a trickle; there is a large and growing net transfer of financial resources (nearly $30 billion last year) from poor people and poor countries to relatively rich countries and relatively rich people; the catch phrases of the day are "policy reform," "structural adjustment," "conditionality" and "austerity."

This, in our summary view, is the historical record. The prescriptions of the Brandt Commission—and most others being considered now—are either macroeconomic solutions which do not take the human element adequately into consideration or Band-Aids (some of them quite large) which treat only the symptoms or efforts to lighten the debt burden so that these countries can buy our exports. As we wrote in our pastoral letter, however, the Third World debt crisis reveals a more fundamental systemic problem. What happened in the 1980s, like what happened in the decade before it, resulted not only from policy but from structure. . . .

"The creditor institutions in particular must share the burden."

For many of us who are concerned with this problem of Third World debt, there is the further complication of how at least some of the borrowed money was spent. It is documented, for example, that capital flight from Third World countries has increased, as ruling and economic elites transferred funds into high-interest-paying accounts and investments in the industrialized countries. (I do not need to bore you with examples, since they are only too obvious.) The very banks that are paying interest on the foreign accounts of those elites are obtaining much of the money to do so by further penalizing and taxing workers and farmers in developing countries that are meeting their debt-service burden. Then when, as in 1982, a major country gets into difficulty, the banks either cease lending (but continue to insist on payment and therefore earn profits) or are cajoled into rescheduling loans, for which they increase the spread between the interest they pay on deposits and the interest they collect on the loans (and charge high fees for doing it).

It seems to us that the injustice in these circumstances is rather clear: First, poor people in poor countries are forced to pay back debts pushed on their not uneager but often unrepresentative governments by profit-seeking banks in the industrialized world; second, poor countries which shored up the industrialized world after the first oil shock, but could not do so after the second, are now required to continue—and in fact, increase—the net transfer of resources to the relatively rich North; third, workers and farmers in countries like the United States are losing jobs, income and assets because their former customers either cannot afford to buy their products in view of the required debt repayments or are competing in those very markets in order to earn foreign exchange to pay back the debts; fourth, the bulk of this debt is interest, not principal. (Some, particularly in the Third World, ask whether the front loading of interest in these circumstances could be considered usury.)

One Step Further

A Joint Economic Committee report of last May, [1986] for example, estimated that U.S. agricultural exports to Latin America declined one-third, prices of exported farm commodities fell about 20 percent and competing grain exports from Latin America more than doubled—all because of the debt crisis of that region. The Brandt Commission was quite right to say all countries must share the burden. We would take it one step further: The creditor institutions in particular must share the burden.

In the midst of this malfunctioning system the IMF rose to quick and unexpected prominence in 1982. Originally established to provide short-term credit to countries that were having difficulties with their balance of payments, the IMF found its time frame unexpectedly lengthened because of the systemic problems that were emerging—and thus was pushed into the role of a development agency. But the IMF's standard formula for meeting the short-term liquidity problems did not change: Devalue the currency to encourage exports by lowering their price and thus earn foreign exchange; hold the line on wage increases to reduce the incentive to consume (and thus compete with exports); and cut consumer subsidies and public services to reduce inflation and the budget deficit. . . .

Creditor Sacrifices

We are pleased to see that pundits, politicians and even some bankers are beginning to recognize that the creditors must accept a share of the sacrifices needed to resolve the Third World debt crisis. We believe, however, that it is reasonable to look carefully at two kinds of debt problems at least. The first is that of mainly Latin American countries, which account for "roughly 40 percent of the total external debt of all capital-importing countries." Between 1981 and 1983, according to the IMF, net commercial lending to Latin America dropped from

$55 billion to $1 billion, import volume decreased by 40 percent, unemployment rose and for all practical purposes growth stopped. We have noted the dramatic announcements and actions by Mexico, Brazil and Argentina. These events seem to us to be one more set of clear indications that the policies followed up to this point, in addition to being unfair, are also ineffective.

The debt of sub-Saharan Africa poses a quite different problem. The bulk of it is owed not to commercial banks, but to governments or to the multilateral institutions created by governments—the World Bank, the regional banks and the IMF. As we pointed out in our pastoral letter, ["Economic Justice for All"] "although their aggregate debt of about $100 billion is only a quarter that of Latin America, their collateral (oil, minerals, manufactures, grain, etc.) is much less adequate, their ability to service external debt much weaker and the possibility of their rescheduling it very small." In this case we believe that "forgiveness," perhaps in the guise of converting this official debt to a local-currency obligation to be paid into a development bank in the country, would be an appropriate and effective solution. Criteria for such conversion would, of course, have to be very carefully studied. . . .

Imposing Hardships

A contribution to the debt debate is the publication of the Pontifical Commission for Justice and Peace, "At the Service of the Human Community: An Ethical Approach to the International Debt Question." In his introductory Presentation Cardinal Roger Etchegaray, President of the commission, after summarizing the history of the crisis in much the same terms the U.S. bishops used, writes: "When credit agencies consider the situation solely from the economic and monetary angle, they often impose on the debtor countries terms, in exchange for accrued credit, that can contribute, at least in the short term, to unemployment, recession and a drastic reduction in the standard of living. This causes suffering, first of all for the poorest as well as for certain sectors of the middle class. In brief, it is a situation that is intolerable and, in the medium term, disastrous for the creditors themselves. Debt servicing cannot be met at the price of the asphyxiation of a country's economy, and no government can morally demand of its people privations incompatible with human dignity. . . . Economic structures and financial mechanisms are at the service of the human person and not vice versa."

The first of thc ethical principles enunciated by the Vatican document is the very term used by the managing director of the IMF in his speech quoted above: co-responsibility. Both the U.S. bishops' letter and the Vatican document emphasize that "in order to be just, interdependence should give rise to new

and broader expressions of solidarity which respect the equal dignity of all peoples. . . . Solidarity implies an awareness and acceptance of co-responsibility for the causes and the solutions relative to international debt. . . . The various partners must agree on an equitable sharing of the adjustment efforts and the necessary sacrifices, taking into account the priority to be given to the needs of the most deprived peoples. It is the responsibility of the countries that are better off to assure a larger share" ("An Ethical Approach").

The pontifical commission's document spreads this co-responsibility rather widely: "Due to their greater economic power, the industrialized countries bear a heavier responsibility, which they must acknowledge and accept." (Politicians are called on specifically to form public opinion in this area.)

"Due to their greater economic power, the industrialized countries bear a heavier [debt] responsibility, which they must acknowledge and accept."

Groups in authority in indebted countries must be willing "to explain their own actions, errors and even abuses" and avoid the temptation to "shift full responsibility to other countries" so that they will not have "to propose any changes which would affect them directly." They must also "accept having their actions and any responsibilities they may have in their countries' indebtedness scrutinized (and must) . . . promote sustained economic growth . . . in order to ensure a broader and more just distribution among all."

Though "creditors have rights, acknowledged by the debtors . . . , creditor states have to find reimbursement conditions which are compatible with each debtor state's ability to meet its basic needs."

Ethical Banking

Commercial banks are urged to finance "projects on the basis of their impact on growth in preference to 'safer' projects with more immediate investment returns," even though this approach "goes beyond the traditional function of commercial banks insofar as it invites them to undertake a type of discernment which transcends the ordinary criteria of profitability."

"Multinational companies have extensive economic, financial and technological power. . . . As economic and financial actors on the international stage, they are called to co-responsibility and solidarity which is above and beyond their own vested interests."

Finally, the multilateral financial organizations "are faced with new and urgent responsibilities: to help solve the debt crisis of the developing countries, to avoid a generalized collapse of the international financial system; to help all peoples, especially those in greatest need, to bring about their own development; to combat the spread of poverty under all its various forms and thereby promote peace by eliminating the threats of conflicts."

The link which the Vatican document establishes between a just solution of the debt problem and social peace is crucially important. Although the debt crisis has coincided with—or perhaps even partially caused—considerable democratization in Latin America during the last few years as mismanagement by authoritarian ruling groups was revealed, there is a danger that the austerity associated with IMF standby agreements and commercial bank pressure for full repayment may push these fledgling democracies to adopt unpopular policies that could lead to a revival of authoritarianism to enforce the austerity programs. Thus the banks may be pitting themselves unwittingly against the very forces in the debtor countries that could provide a democratic growth-with-equity alternative.

Our discussion here, as well as much of the analytic material in our pastoral letter, has a dispassionate, even clinical, tone. We hear a different voice in letters from American missionaries overseas, like one that came in describing the missionary's return to the mission country after some period of time: "Today I rode the bus downtown, for which I paid 250,000 pesos. . . . When I was here 10 years ago, I could have bought the bus for that price."

Passionate Debate

We also hear a different voice when we meet with Latin American bishops on these issues as we did in Miami. The "cool" analysis of the debt problem became immediate, personal, passionate and urgent when we heard a Brazilian bishop say, for example: "Your debt is an iron ring around the necks of my people." These bishops had two major financial problems on their minds—the debt and capital flight. They were very hard on their own political and economic leaders for pushing money out of the country into those attractive overseas investments, but almost equally hard on the industrialized countries for placing those profit temptations in the paths of the elites.

I worry a little about the almost exclusive focus on the debt problem, as well as about the tendency to view it in tandem with the trade problem—as if to suggest that the main or only reason for relieving the debt burden is to make it possible for the debtor countries to buy our exports. We do not believe the Third World debt problem can be solved without addressing all aspects of the international order. We said in our pastoral letter on the economy that "we believe that U.S. policy toward the developing world

should reflect our traditional regard for human rights and our concern for social progress. In economic policy, as we noted in our pastoral letter on nuclear war, the major international economic relationships of aid, trade, finance and investment are interdependent among themselves and illustrate the range of interdependence issues facing U.S. policy. . . . Each relationship offers us the possibility of substantial positive movement toward increasing social justice in the developing world."

In the debt area as with the other three—trade, aid and investment—the problem goes beyond even the system itself. "It afflicts and oppresses large numbers of people who are already severely disadvantaged. That is the scandal: It is the poorest people who suffer most from the austerity measures required when a country seeks the IMF 'seal of approval,' which establishes its creditworthiness for a commercial loan (or perhaps an external aid program). It is these same people who suffer most when commodity prices fall, when food cannot be imported or they cannot buy it, and when natural disasters occur. Our commitment to the preferential option for the poor does not permit us to remain silent in these circumstances."

"Responsibility for the solution must be shared in an equitable fashion . . . and the [debt] burden must be lifted from the poor."

We are aware that neither of our two pastoral letters prescribes a policy solution to the problems it focuses on. We think that is proper. The virtue of prudence enters the equation as soon as one moves beyond the realm of principle. We see these two letters as inextricably linked; peace is, after all, the fruit of justice. We know that just as what the peace pastoral recommended in a general sense would call for a very different policy than the United States is following, so would the economic pastoral. But just as one effect of the peace pastoral was to identify the Roman Catholic community with the effort to reverse the arms race and stem the dangerous drift toward nuclear war, one effect of the economic pastoral will, we hope, be to identify the Roman Catholic community with the cause of economic justice—especially for the poor, both in the United States and in the Third World.

Suggested Solutions

How that objective is to be achieved is, of course, a matter of debate on many issues. One of them—possibly the most urgent and intransigent—is the question we are discussing.

Even though we don't have a formula to propose to you, we would like to suggest several principles which we and many other religious groups believe should underlie a normative approach to a solution to the problem of Third World debt:

1. Responsibility for the solution must be shared in an equitable fashion by both creditors and debtor countries, and the burden must be lifted from the poor.

2. The primary objective of any approach must be to improve the quality of life of the poorest people through restored and equitably shared economic growth, not to preserve the profitability of banks.

3. Criteria for adjustment of each country's debt situation should take into account, among other things, what the money was borrowed for, how it was used, what efforts the debtor country has already made or begun to repay it, and how the debtor nation proposes to stop capital flight.

4. Efforts to resolve the short-term debt problems should be undertaken in close association with a very basic look at the entire international financial system, with a view to systemic changes designed to establish more equitable arrangements that can prevent the recurrence of this kind of crisis.

5. Any structural adjustment or other debt-solution package must preserve the basic human rights of the citizens of the debtor country and the integrity of its government.

6. Any viable solution must recognize and relieve external factors beyond the control of the debtor country that tend to aggravate and perpetuate the burden—interest rates, commodity prices, trade barriers, budget deficits, etc.

Rembert Weakland is the Catholic Archbishop of Milwaukee.

Debtor Nations Must Help End the World Debt Crisis

James S. Henry

The toppling of Ferdinand Marcos and Baby Doc Duvalier has focused attention on the wealth that Third World oligarchs have plundered and stashed abroad. The collapse of oil has left countries like Mexico and Venezuela begging for relief from their debts. These two stories—capital flight and international debt—are part of the same story. In some cases, the wealthiest classes of poor countries have actually sent more money out of their countries than foreign borrowing has brought in—and often it's the same money. American banks have promoted, and profited from, both sides of the transaction. Sometimes the money never even leaves the United States. The entire cycle is completed with a few bookkeeping entries in New York.

More than half of the money borrowed by Mexico, Venezuela, and Argentina during the last decade has effectively flowed right back out the door, often the same year or even month it flowed in. Indeed, there are already enough private foreign assets owned by the citizens of major debtor nations to go a long way toward servicing their countries' foreign debts. The most aggressive banks, such as Citibank, have probably accumulated almost as much in assets from poor countries as they have loaned to them. Their real role has been to take funds that Third World elites have stolen from their governments and to loan them back, earning a nice spread each way.

American government policies make it far too easy to transfer and hide financial assets. As a result, the U.S. itself is one of the world's largest tax havens, and the largest for Latin America. Indeed, because of such policies the U.S. is actually a net *debtor* of Latin American countries.

It all comes down to one of the largest wealth transfers in history, with a few thousand affluent families and their retainers cackling all the way to the bank, the poor people of these countries indentured for years to work off the debts, the bankers playing a clever double game, and American taxpayers expected to subsidize bailouts that make the 1975 New York City debt crisis look like a rounding error. This is the *real* story of the "debt crisis": the story of what happened to all the money.

The *"Sacadolares"*

Consider Mexico. On March 6, [1986], a Mexico City newspaper published a list of 575 names of Mexican nationals, each of whom has at least one million dollars in deposits with foreign banks. The exposure of these *"sacadolares"*—people who take out dollars—caused an uproar because it comes just as Mexico is once again pleading bankruptcy to its international bankers and the U.S. Treasury. Mexico maintains that it needs another six billion to ten billion dollars of new foreign loans and interest subsidies this year to avert insolvency. This would be the second major bailout for Mexico in the last three years.

One example of the *"sacadolares"* may be the president of Mexico himself, Miguel de la Madrid. A Harvard-bred technocrat, de la Madrid was annointed by the previous president, Lopez Portillo, whom he had served as minister of budget. He had never before held elective office. (But then some say that no one really holds elective office in Mexico.)

Portillo was a stout law professor whose regime was distinguished by profligate spending, wildly optimistic growth plans, and corruption that was unprecedented even by Mexican standards. All of this was paid for on time. Between 1978 and 1982 the country's foreign debt more than doubled, to $85 billion. Today it approaches $100 billion, one of the highest debt levels per dollar of national income in the world. Very little of this money went into productive investments. Billions were squandered on

James S. Henry, "Where the Money Went," *The New Republic*, April 14, 1986. Reprinted by permission of THE NEW REPUBLIC, © 1986, The New Republic, Inc.

noncompetitive steel plants, a six-billion-dollar nuclear power plant that still doesn't function, a gas pipeline to nowhere, wasteful development loans, arms, and payoffs to contractors and public officials. (Portillo, who moved to Rome after leaving office, is widely rumored to have absconded with over one billion dollars.)

Wasted Money

Western bankers looked the other way as their money was wasted. The loan fees were lucrative, and many of the banks' corporate customers were making bundles on these "white elephants." The banks also complacently assumed that the U.S. government would never allow either Mexico or Citibank to go bankrupt. Furthermore, until 1981 or so, no one at any particular bank knew just how much money the *other* banks were lending to Mexico.

De la Madrid's first promise when he took office was to seek a "moral renovation" and rebuild the confidence of Mexico's investors. He lectured the nation on the need for "belt-tightening." Unemployment grew to over 30 percent and real wages sank to 1963 levels. It was thus a little embarrassing that just as de la Madrid arrived on his first official visit to Washington in May 1984, Jack Anderson revealed a secret U.S. intelligence report that de la Madrid himself had been accumulating substantial deposits in a Swiss bank account—at least $162 million during 1983 alone. (The deposits were transferred by wire—the National Security Agency had been listening. The *New York Times* subsequently confirmed the story.) The State Department issued a curious statement that the "U.S. government applauds President de la Madrid's commitment to addressing the issue of honesty in government."

"Argentina's capital outflow during this decade was over 60 percent of its foreign borrowing."

There is no way to know exactly how much capital has left Mexico. Banks naturally try to keep the figures secret. But there are two accounting techniques that enable us to make indirect estimates. One is to measure the discrepancy between net exports of goods and services and net imports of capital. The difference ought to reflect net short-term capital flows, and subtracting the known capital imports should give us a rough figure for the unknown capital exports. All of these figures are inexact. (Cynics note that Mexico's official balance-of-payments statistics overlook both its biggest import, arms, and its second-biggest export, drugs.)

But in the case of Mexico, a second method of calculation produces surprisingly similar results. This is simply to take all the money that's known to have flowed in from abroad, subtract the known ways it's been put to use, and assume that the rest flowed back out again.

Both methods indicate that capital flight soared during the Portillo years, especially from 1979 to 1981, just as Mexico's foreign debt was exploding. For example, in 1981, while Mexico was taking on about $20 billion in new foreign debt from commercial banks, capital flight was nine billion dollars to $11 billion. After 1981, capital flight started to decline: there was just not that much more to take out. Growth in new debt also stopped. Over the years from 1974 to 1985, Mexico borrowed $97 billion and sent about half—$50 billion—right back out again. Things were even worse elsewhere. Argentina's capital outflow during this decade was over 60 percent of its foreign borrowing, and in Venezuela there was virtually a dollar-for-dollar offset. In contrast, Brazilians (11 percent) and even Marcos' cronies in the Philippines (25 percent) were much less aggressive in moving capital out of their countries.

Capital Outflow

Hidden capital exports are only part of the story, since these private investments have grown in value since leaving Mexico. Many Mexicans prefer investing abroad in very short-term assets, especially bank time deposits and Treasury bills. These are safe, highly liquid, untaxed, and simple. The volume of U.S. bank time deposits owned by foreigners has grown dramatically in the past few years, driven by Latin American flight capital. The Mexicans are the largest single source. Private bankers and investment advisers who serve this market say that probably two-thirds or more of Mexican flight capital has found its way into time deposits. Now, these experts say, some large Mexican depositors have begun to shift their holdings into U.S. government securities, because of concern about the health of U.S. banks that have loaned too much money to places like Mexico!

Making some reasonable assumptions about the return on these investments, and also assuming that no taxes have been paid—either to the U.S., because there is no tax owed on "portfolio interest" earned by nonresidents, or to Mexico, because of outright tax evasion—we can estimate how much Mexican flight capital is now abroad. These calculations are subject to all sorts of qualifications. But if they are even close to being accurate, they suggest that by 1984 the value of Mexican flight capital exceeded the face value of all commercial bank loans to Mexico, and by 1985 it was closing in on the face value of the country's total external debt. Since these tattered loans to places like Mexico are actually worth far less than their face value, it seems quite likely that Mexico is actually a net creditor. As one Federal Reserve Board member said recently, "The problem is not that Latin Americans don't have assets. They do. The problem is, they're all in Miami."

The U.S. banks' share of loans to the major Latin American debtors has been less than 30 percent. By contrast, our share of the private flight capital from these nations is rumored to be 70 to 80 percent for Mexico and Venezuela, and 50 to 60 percent for Brazil and Argentina. This means that the U.S. as a whole is almost certainly a net debtor of all of these countries, except possibly Brazil. U.S. banks now have about $26 billion in outstanding loans to Mexico. Estimating the accumulated value of Mexican capital-flight wealth at $85 billion by 1984, and assuming that 70 percent is invested here, Mexicans have at least $30 billion more socked away in U.S. banks than Mexico owes to U.S. banks. Total direct investment by all U.S. firms in Mexico, by contrast, was six billion dollars in 1984. Similar calculations for the other Latin American major countries yield a total net balance in favor of the U.S. of $40 billion to $60 billion in 1984. By now [1986] the figure may exceed $70 billion. Again, these figures are conservative because they are based on comparing the dubious face value of the debts with the market value of the assets. In the case of Mexico, estimated annual earnings on these assets are already over three-quarters of the annual interest owed on Mexico's foreign debt.

The U.S. Treasury polls American banks, security dealers, and other businesses on their financial transactions with foreigners. These data are riddled with imperfections, most of which lead to underestimates. Still, they do show patterns that are consistent with other things we know. They indicate that between 1978 and 1985 Latin Americans and their Caribbean tax-haven proxies increased their short-term deposits with U.S. banks by at least $33 billion. At the same time U.S. banks were increasing their loans to Latin America by about $50 billion. Thus the basic role played by U.S. banks to Latin America was that of a middleman between the short-term deposits of the countries' elites and the medium-term loans demanded by their governments.

"Dollarization"

Another very important category of U.S. assets that Latin Americans have been stocking up on is cash. This is a "foreign asset" that is often physically kept at home. From a financial standpoint, it represents a net claim that foreigners have on the U.S. There is no direct measure of U.S. cash held abroad, but "dollarization" is rampant in Argentina, Brazil, and Mexico. It is common practice for people to squirrel away whole suitcases of $100 bills as hedge against depreciation of the local currency. This helps to account for the curious fact that there are now about three $100 bills in circulation for each man, woman, and child in the United States. A recent U.S. Treasury "guesstimate" is that perhaps $20 billion worth of them are offshore.

Cash is also a preferred method of transferring money from local to foreign accounts. Venezuelans traveling to Miami reported over two billion dollars of cash in 1981 alone on the Treasury forms that entrants to the U.S. have to fill out. Currency has long poured into the Miami Federal Reserve district because of drug traffic. More recently, though, the El Paso and San Antonio Federal Reserve districts have reported net receipts of currency, reflecting the large cash deposits that Mexicans have been carrying across the border. The explosive growth of San Francisco's receipts during the past two years is apparently a combination of Philippine flight capital and a shift of drug money to the West Coast.

"The problem is not that Latin Americans don't have assets. They do. The problem is, they're all in Miami."

Who owns these assets? The typical Mexican investor with dollars at home or abroad is really pretty middle class. As one writer recently put it, "Even the Mexico City shoe-shine boys stockpile dollars." But even if everyone has a bit of it, the key fact about flight capital is that it is highly concentrated. At the very top are the bankers' wet dream, the superrich. These are the people of Citibank's "Global Elite," a list of 5,000 or so people from around the world who are supposed to have individual net worths greater than $100 million. The U.S. supposedly has about 500 to 600 such people, depending on the state of the stock market. In the Latin American context, these people include a lot of names most Americans—and indeed, most of their own countrymen, given their taste for discretion—have never heard of, but they are fabulously rich. These are the happy few that automatically qualify for services like the new American Express "Black Card," the ultra VIP credit card that has a credit line of $500,000 and offers services such as private planes, bodyguards, and access to Fifth Avenue stores in the wee hours of the morning for "solo shopping." Obviously at this level the key function of the card is not credit, but identity: "Do you know me? I may look like a twit, but I own Paraguay."

Meanwhile, Mexico's income per capita averages less than $2,000 a year. And since 1982, the debt problem has made things worse. Imports and domestic spending have been slashed to meet the interest bill. For the lower half of the population, this means that real incomes have fallen further from their already low base.

How did Third World elites manage to convert all that foreign debt capital into private foreign assets? There are several explanations that are not mutually exclusive. The "innocent bystander" view holds that the local rich just happened to deploy their own assets abroad at precisely the time their governments chose to borrow heavily abroad to finance attempts at growth. Of course a more sensible approach would have been to fund public spending with taxes or direct foreign investment in the local economy. But local elites are so powerful that serious income or wealth taxes are almost unheard of, while domestic enterprise is protected by a host of barriers against foreign investment.

Furthermore, local elites do not just react passively to the local governments. In many cases they *are* the local governments, or at least the executive committees. Thus a basic method of taking money out of Mexico has been to exploit overvalued official exchange rates with the help of foreign banks. The preservation of this exchange rate system even in the face of massive capital flight is very hard to understand unless we take into account the profits made from it by people in positions to influence policy.

"How did Third World elites manage to convert all that foreign debt capital into private foreign assets?"

There's also, of course, plenty of outright graft in converting dollars borrowed by government projects into private wealth. The actual pathways are endless: phony intermediary companies that recontract with foreign suppliers on public projects and take a hefty spread; importers who get permits to purchase foreign exchange for imports that either never get bought or are wildly over-invoiced; developers who get public loans for projects that don't exist; local "consultants" who are paid by U.S. suppliers in New York dollar accounts, and so on.

To what extent were American bankers aware of what was going on? It's a nice question. Some observers feel they must have been knowing, or at least willing, participants, just like the middlemen in phony-asset scams throughout financial history. This suspicion requires an assumption about the intelligence, cunning, and foresight of bankers that, in my experience, is not warranted. What's indisputable is that when wealthy Mexicans invest their own capital abroad, they are much more cautious than the foreign bankers who financed all their country's debt.

It's also indisputable that leading American banks are as involved in ferrying capital out of Mexico as they were in lending money to the country in the first place. The U.S. banks that are the most active in "international private banking" to wealthy Mexicans are Citibank, Morgan Guaranty, Bank of America, and Chase, plus several large regional banks in Texas and California. They all serve a key client list of at least several hundred wealthy Mexican customers. They all have very active calling programs designed to recruit new clients. They all play an active role in helping wealthy Mexicans get their money out of the country. They all help such customers design sophisticated offshore trusts and investment companies to shelter income from taxes and political exposure. They all try very hard to keep the identity of their customers a secret. They are all more or less actively involved in lobbying U.S. authorities to preserve policies toward taxation, bank regulation, and bank secrecy that are favorable to their clients.

Money Transfers

"When we go in there," one international private banker told me about his trips to the Third World, "we're not taking any kind of information with us, and when we leave the country we don't have any papers with us either. You know, I tell [my boss] when I leave on a trip to remember my face if anything happens to me. But he says, don't worry, the bank will never admit that you were a part of us."

"Pouch" services or their equivalents—helping clients move money secretly—are among the most important services that private bankers provide. If handled discreetly this can be a real competitive advantage, because among other things the bank learns enough about a customer's "private parts" to lock him in. The standard image of money-laundering is a bunch of shady characters trucking suitcases of cash through airports and depositing it in obscure banks in the Caymans, Florida, the Bahamas, or Switzerland. Although some of this obviously goes on, especially at the "drug-related" end of the business, this is not really first-class money-laundering at all. One banker described to me the challenge of helping rich clients to get money out of Mexico without leaving a trail: "You can buy dollars in Mexico from the Central Bank, no problem. The problem is that you are basically registering yourself, exactly what you don't want. You could go to a local bank, buy a $100,000 check there with pesos, and then send it to the States. But then when you deposit that check, it's going to show [what account] it went to. So what happens is . . . the customer would go to his own bank, draw a cashier's check in the name of [XYZ Foreign Bank], and deposit that in an [XYZ Foreign Bank] account. So his name is not on that check at all. Or deposits are made in a customer's peso account in a Mexican branch of a U.S. bank, and credits are made to the customer's dollar account in New York." Since November 1985 the Mexican government has restricted the use of the foreign banks' "peso windows" in Mexico in order to curtail such transfers. However, the more aggressive banks have already begun to help their private customers evade even this restriction by setting up parallel foreign exchange swaps that avoid the banking system entirely, leaving virtually no records. Again, the major banks have played a central role in disarming the new restrictions.

Clever Bankers

The really clever private bankers also have devised methods so that Mexicans can use their foreign capital without leaving home, much less being taxed on it by their own governments. The favorite method is the so-called "back-to-back" loan, whereby the bank "loans" the client his own money. This not only reduces the client's taxes even further, but helps him take more money out of the country.

These international private bankers are not malevolent or obtuse. They are doing exactly what they get paid to do. Theirs is not a labor of love, but a very profitable business, with returns on assets of two to three percent and pretax returns on equity of 100 percent and more. In an era when most other low-cost sources of bank funds have dried up, private banking to Third World countries looks pretty good. In fact, this was just how lending to Third World governments looked in the 1970s, relative to commercial, retail, or housing lending at home.

Citibank is clearly the most aggressive American bank in international private banking ("IPB"). It appears to have over 1,500 people dedicated to this activity worldwide, and over $26 billion in IPB assets. . . .

"Countries like Mexico should get no more money until they have enacted reforms to ensure that the dollars we lend them don't come right back again."

Overall, at least half of Citibank's $26 billion or so in IPB assets probably belongs to Latin Americans. This compares with Citibank's total loan exposure to the "Big Four"—Brazil, Mexico, Argentina, and Venezuela—of about $10.3 billion. Thus, even allowing for loans to the rest of Latin America, Citibank probably comes very close to owing more money to Latin Americans than it is owed.

Banks are required to report large loans outstanding to individual countries. But there is no requirement to report the country origins of private banking assets. This secrecy is probably no accident. In the case of several major banks and other financial institutions, the truth might be a little embarrassing—they are not really net lenders to these countries at all. The aggregate balance of loans and deposits is a little clearer. Our best estimate is that U.S. banks as a whole probably now manage international private banking assets of roughly $100 billion to $120 billion, 60 to 70 percent of which comes from Latin American private banking assets, compared to total U.S. bank loans outstanding to Latin America of about $83 billion. Not only is the U.S. economy as a whole probably a net debtor of Latin America: our commercial banks alone are close to being net debtors of Latin America.

But this is the kind of debtor anyone would love to be. Combining what we know about capital flight and private lending, a reasonable estimate of the banks' profits on the "round-trip" for Mexico alone is $2.4 billion in 1984. On an equity base of four billion dollars, that's a return of 70 percent. One can quibble about the precise assumptions behind such estimates, but the basic findings are robust. U.S. banks have so far reaped a bonanza from their own disastrous international lending policies of the last decade.

Third World Solutions

As Third World leaders and international bankers warm up for another chorus of moaning about the debt crisis, they need a forcible reminder that the solution may lie in their own hands. Countries like Mexico should get no more money until they have enacted reforms to ensure that the dollars we lend them don't come right back again in the bank accounts of rich private citizens. The United States should take steps of its own to correct policies that encourage capital flight—especially laws that make us a haven for foreigners flouting their own nations' tax systems. Finally, international banks must take responsibility for the impact that "international private banking" is having on the poor nations where it operates. The easier it is for these nations' ruling elites to smuggle assets abroad, the less incentive there is to clean up at home. The capital flight these banks are promoting and facilitating in the 1980s is just as irresponsible as the loans they were peddling in the 1970s.

James S. Henry is a New York economist.

Writing Off Loans Would Help End the Debt Crisis

Marc Levinson

The lingering trade deficit has finally brought the Third World's debt problem home to corporate America. After half a decade of watching Mexico and Zaire, Brazil and the Philippines joust with bankers over one rescheduling plan after another, business has come to understand that the $750 billion foreign debt of less developed countries is not just the bankers' problem.

But the search for a solution quickly runs up against one unpleasant fact: Dealing seriously with the debt means writing off at least a portion of the billions of dollars owed to U.S. banks. Increasingly, scholars of the debt situation contend that without debt relief there is little chance that the debtor countries, particularly in Latin America, will again become significant markets for U.S. exports.

None of the austerity measures and emergency loan programs pasted together since the onset of Mexico's debt crisis in 1982 has done the trick. "We've been at it for five years now and the situation is no better," says economist Stanley Fischer of the Massachusetts Institute of Technology. "The countries have paid significantly. At some point, you have to say 'enough.'"

An Unpopular Solution

The case for write-offs is still unpopular in Washington, where Congressmen rightly worry about explaining to constituents why loans to Peruvian manufacturers should be forgiven while loans to Iowa farmers are not. But as the debt crisis becomes a seemingly permanent feature of the economic landscape, outright opposition to debt relief is beginning to crumble.

The stakes for business are large. Although the Reagan Administration has viewed it primarily as a threat to the stability of the financial system, the debt has had disastrous consequences for American manufacturers. One hard-pressed debtor country after another has slashed imports to conserve foreign exchange. At the same time, by devaluing currencies, subsidizing key industries and tying permits to import essential material to increased exports, the debtor nations have increased their penetration of markets abroad.

The heavy international lending in the late 1970s and early 1980s was a boon to U.S. business, as cash-rich Third World countries stocked up on production machinery, generating equipment and other U.S. products. But as U.S. interest rates took off in 1979, those floating-rate loans became far more costly than the borrowers had anticipated. Meanwhile, commodity prices fell precipitously, confronting almost every developing country with a payments crunch.

"In the [developing countries'] frustration to finance themselves, they want to be net exporting nations," observes Colby H. Chandler, chairman of Eastman Kodak Co. "They feel if they force every multinational [located in the Third World] to export, they will be on their way. That means that a company such as ours is being forced into businesses that are not our strength in order to have something to export."

The Debt Burden

U.S. exports to the developing countries have been hurt not only by such government measures to manage trade flows, but by slow economic growth stemming from the need to allocate scarce dollars to debt service. In most Latin American countries, per capita income in 1985 was lower than it had been in 1981, hardly a situation conducive to strong demand for imports. As a result, the $5.5 billion U.S. trade surplus with Latin America in 1981 fell to a $16 billion deficit by 1984. U.S. exports to the region, which peaked at $39 billion in 1981, have been in the $27 billion range for three years. U.S. imports, which amounted to $33.5 billion six years ago, have exceeded $40 billion since 1984.

Despite this severe blow to manufacturers, both the U.S. government and international financial institutions have treated debt service as a given. Their basic assumption is that the debtor countries *must* pay their debts, and that the industrialized countries must accommodate their need to run trade surpluses in order to keep debt service current. In practice, this has meant that everything from Venezuelan steel to Brazilian airplanes and Korean automobiles has flooded into the U.S. Nearly 60% of the Third World's exports in 1986 were absorbed by the U.S., versus only 7% by Japan.

No Threat of Collapse

Today, the prospect of the financial system's collapse has receded. Most European banks have quietly set aside reserves, while U.S. banks have simply allowed their outstanding developing country credits to become a diminishing portion of their asset bases. A major default now would be an unpleasantness, not a catastrophe. Barring a prolonged recession in the industrial world, the ritual of threatened defaults and last-minute renegotiations is likely to continue indefinitely.

American manufacturers, however, continue to pay a heavy price. The careful arrangements to keep both banks and debtor countries solvent require the latter to run trade surpluses for years to come. Korea, Mexico and other industrializing nations will continue to flood the U.S. with ever more sophisticated products, while those countries' markets remain blocked to U.S. goods.

"The basic principle is simple: Everybody involved—bankers, creditors and debtor countries—should bear some of the losses."

That is why, at long last, attention in Washington has turned to a basic restructuring of the debt situation. Affirms New Jersey Senator Bill Bradley, whose Senate Finance Subcommittee on International Debt will debate the matter: "We must give the Third World interest rate and debt relief to generate American jobs."

Two major proposals to alleviate the debt burden are under discussion on Capitol Hill. Bradley seeks a global approach. The basic principle is simple: Everybody involved—bankers, creditors and debtor countries—should bear some of the losses. He links bank forgiveness of some loans and lower interest spreads on others with increased lending by the World Bank and the International Monetary Fund,

economic reforms in debtor nations and measures to open LDC [less developed country] markets to U.S. goods. "A lot of thoughtful people feel Bradley has a point," says Lawrence Fox, vice president for international economic affairs of the National Association of Manufacturers. "I'm not sure it's a good idea to cancel debt, but you can accomplish the same thing by stretching it out."

A less drastic alternative, originally put forth by Princeton University professor Peter Kenen and now promoted by Senator Paul Sarbanes and Representative David Obey, calls for Japan and West Germany to fund a new international venture that would buy Third World debt from commercial banks at a discount. By reducing the value of the outstanding debt and cutting the number of creditors involved, the Sarbanes-Obey plan would simplify a long-term restructuring of the debt burden.

The debate in Congress will serve more to keep the Administration's feet to the fire than to pass legislation. A comprehensive solution to the debt problem is too complex to legislate. Says one Senate staffer: "Congress can exhort and even direct the Administration, but beyond that there's not a lot Congress can do."

Piecemeal Solutions

The Reagan Administration, which was slow to admit the connection between debt and trade in the first place, has discouraged the search for global solutions. Instead, it has dealt with each country's urgent problems in a deliberately piecemeal fashion. The Baker Plan, announced by Treasury Secretary James Baker in 1985, rejects measures to reduce the debt loads of developing countries. Instead, it emphasizes economic reforms and more lending by the World Bank, the IMF, and private bankers.

In addition, the Administration has sought to spread the burden of trade deficits by encouraging faster growth and more open markets in Europe and Japan. "The debt strategies bouncing around on the Hill are well-intended but generally counterproductive," argues Charles Dallara, deputy assistant secretary of the treasury for international affairs and the U.S. director of the IMF. "You can have a broad strategy, but it's not realistic to attempt to negotiate a basket of tradeoffs with a large group of debtors in a broad multilateral setting."

The case-by-case approach has successfully staved off defaults by the major debtor countries. It has not, however, materially improved the ability of any country to handle its debts on a long-term basis. Even fast-growing Brazil, until recently the shining example of a country that would soon outgrow its $108 billion debt, found itself in trouble again after a precipitous drop in its trade surplus.

In reality, there are only three ways to ease the debt burdens of developing countries in the forseeable future. One is a sharp increase in the prices of sugar, copper and other export commodities—a highly improbable development. The second is a further fall in interest rates. The remaining option is to forgive part of the debt.

Already, bank loans to many Third World countries are selling at an average of 65% of face value on the nascent secondary market, and the prices of bank stocks reflect this. If banks were forced to write off a portion of their loans—a step they frequently take for domestic problem debtors—the developing nations would face far smaller debt service payments. As a result, they could survive with smaller trade surpluses, buying more imported goods to fuel their domestic growth.

Bankers' Rage

Bankers, of course, flush with rage when debt forgiveness is mentioned, and the regulators have been reluctant to force such a step. "It is inappropriate for the government unilaterally to force private financial institutions to sustain losses," Baker contends. Congress, however, may attempt to force the Administration's hand by considering legislation explicitly linking individual banks' reserve requirements to their outstanding Third World loans.

Without a government mandate, no significant debt write-offs by American banks are likely. No bank wants to be the first to forgive debt, because one bank's forgiveness means that all other creditors have a greater chance of being repaid. Only if all banks are forced to act in concert will significant relief for debtors result.

No one advocates that all Third World debt be written off. MIT's Fischer proposes that an average of 35% of the debt's value be written off over a period of years, bringing the debt's value on the books of creditor banks into line with its actual value in the secondary market. Harvard University economist Jeffrey Sachs would achieve the same end by allowing countries whose per capita income has declined more than 15% since 1980 to skip all interest payments for five to ten years—a proposal which, unlike the Fischer plan, avoids channeling relief to Brazil.

An International Tribunal

The creation of an international tribunal with the power to restructure debt is advocated by John Williamson of the Institute for International Economics. The tribunal would focus on low-income countries whose debt service problems are due to unexpected shocks, such as falling commodity prices.

Requiring write-offs on a case-by-case basis would be far easier if regulators press for a restructuring of the banking system, contends Georgetown University economist Gary Hufbauer. "It may help to encourage weak banks to be taken over by strong banks," Hufbauer says. "That may mean letting a Japanese bank buy Bank of America, or letting the Chinese buy more of Marine Midland."

Whatever its form, debt forgiveness would not be as unfair to the banks as it sounds. Despite all the concern about potential defaults, bankers have raked in enormous profits from their floating-rate foreign loans, as real interest rates soared to record levels. One reason for the hefty earnings is that most Third World borrowers were charged relatively high rates of interest, precisely because they were viewed as risky customers.

So far, forgiving the debt has not generated much enthusiasm from manufacturing lobbyists in Washington. Most industrial companies do not want to carry the ball on the issue. The U.S. Chamber of Commerce is only beginning to study the question. . . .

Uncomfortable Businesses

Although by now management is well aware that the debt directly hurts their businesses, many executives don't know what policies to recommend, and others are uncomfortable staking out positions removed from their firms' immediate concerns. "We raise this issue constantly to make sure it is understood in the Administration and on the Hill," says Peter Mulloney, assistant to the chairman of USX Corp. But, Mulloney says, USX will not take a stand on specfic debt-related proposals. . . .

Then, too, debt relief must be introduced gradually to keep pressure on debtor countries to put their economies in order. Although many experts reject the standard adjustment program developed by the IMF, which overemphasizes currency devaluation and rapid elimination of government subsidies, there is wide agreement that debtor countries must take measures to encourage free markets and private investment.

"Without some type of debt write-offs . . . the developing and the industrialized worlds will remain locked together in an embrace of slow growth."

From the American viewpoint, a reduction of import barriers is high on the list of reforms. "This is a good time for Latin America to liberalize," affirms Robert Hormats, a former State Department official now at Goldman Sachs & Co. "If they liberalize now, they won't experience a big surge in imports because the constraint is foreign exchange."

Countries such as Brazil have been unwilling to eliminate import permits, arguing that they need to control imports in order to service their debts. This need is real—but it does not mean that barriers must be used to protect individual industries. As a condition for forgiving debts, the U.S. should insist that countries that must limit imports do so in a way that is not designed to shield specific types of products.

To make a difference, debt forgiveness must involve more than just the banks. Over one-third of the developing countries' debts are owed to governments and multilateral institutions, such as the IMF, which must also take write-offs if these obligations are to be substantially reduced. In practice, this is already occurring, as IMF and World Bank officials privately concede that most loans to sub-Saharan Africa will never be repaid.

The Debt/Trade Link

Explicitly linking debt forgiveness and trade liberalization will be difficult. In the U.S., as in every other country, the two issues fall into different parts of the governmental structure. Debt is a question for finance ministers and central bankers. Trade ministers have no role in the councils of the IMF. Nowhere do officials weigh the bankers' interest in receiving payments against the manufacturers' interest in more balanced trade with the developing world. Shrugs Federal Reserve Governor Robert Heller, "There isn't that much the Fed can do about it."

But the attempt must be made to bring trade concerns to the forefront of international debt negotiations. By itself, forgiving foreign debt is not a solution to the U.S. trade imbalance. But no other solution advanced to date gives the concerns of America's battered manufacturers equal weight with the repayment claims of the banks. Without some type of debt write-offs, Third World markets will remain barred to U.S. exporters, and the developing and the industrialized worlds will remain locked together in an embrace of slow growth.

Marc Levinson writes for Dun's Business Month, *a business and economics magazine.*

"[Debt] swapping can serve as a model
for a lasting and politically acceptable
solution to the debt crisis."

viewpoint **104**

Loan Swapping Would
Help End the Debt Crisis

Richard S. Weinert

Markets work. So President Ronald Reagan and his backers have taught legions of skeptics, and examples keep popping up in unlikely places. One is Third World debt. When the debt crisis arrived in 1982, many analysts—including this writer—foretold dire consequences if forceful action was not taken to write down the value of the debt and give relief to debtor countries. This did not happen. To date, no public entity—creditor-country governments, debtor-country governments, the International Bank for Reconstruction and Development (World Bank), or the International Monetary Fund (IMF)—has taken any specific initiative to reduce debt-service burdens.

Yet markets have not been idle. Despite, or because of, the public policy vacuum, capital markets have begun to adjust. A new secondary market in discounted Latin American and other Third World debt has developed, with big discounts regularly applied to the debt's face value. In fall 1986, for example, Brazilian government debt could be bought for about 75 per cent of its face value; Mexican government debt for about 57 per cent; Philippine, 60 per cent; Argentine, 65 per cent; Chilean, 67 per cent; and Peruvian, 22 per cent. Bolivian and Nicaraguan debt, by contrast, each sold for less than 10 per cent of their face values. These steep discounts believe the claim that the loans are still good, that the debtor countries are merely experiencing some temporary illiquidity. The claim may be true, but the market does not believe it.

Understanding how and why this debt swapping developed and how it works will help reveal whether the practice should be encouraged or restrained. Even more important, it can show how swapping can serve as a model for a lasting and politically acceptable solution to the debt crisis that will help debtors and creditors alike.

The secondary market in debt serves three purposes that feed off each other. First, it enables private banks to readjust their portfolios by shuffling loans around, much as children trade baseball cards. Second, debtor countries encourage investors to use discounted debt to make investments. Third, debtors use the market to retire debt. Shuffling loans reduces risks to the international financial system by permitting individual banks to strengthen their balance sheets. Debtors have benefited by encouraging investment flows and by starting to lighten their debt burdens.

A Growing Market

No one knows exactly how big the market for debt swaps has become. No transactions are publicized, and most banks are very secretive about them. It is clear, however, that the market is still small but growing quite rapidly. It may have totaled about $1 billion in 1984, $3 billion in 1985, and $6 billion in 1986. This trend is likely to continue and presents some challenges and opportunities to the world economy.

Initially, swapping was stimulated by some banks' desires to modify their exposure to troubled debtors. This could be done in several ways. The simplest would be for a bank to sell off its loans to a given country at a discount and register the loss suffered against its earnings. This tack was eventually taken by smaller banks to the extent that they had sufficient profits to absorb the loss or had already written the loans down to the market's discounted values. At first, however, such transactions were modest simply because there were no buyers, even at discounted prices.

Major creditors could not sell loans for two additional reasons. Financially, they could not afford to take the implicit losses. For example, large private banks typically held Latin American debt equal to

Richard S. Weinert, "Swapping Third World Debt." Reprinted with permission from FOREIGN POLICY 65 (Winter 1986-87). Copyright 1986 by the Carnegie Endowment for International Peace.

two to three times their capital. To register a loss of even 25 per cent of that portfolio would imply wiping out one-half to three-fourths of their capital. This was clearly impossible. Moreover, the political consequences would have been unbearable. The world's big banks had painstakingly forged cooperative links on the debt issue that served all of their interests. For one bank to break ranks and try to dump its debt would have threatened those links and shaken international banking and capital markets.

Accounting gimmickry came to the rescue. By exchanging, or swapping, the debt of one country for that of another, banks could reduce or even eliminate their exposure in some countries without registering any loss. The key to this sleight of hand was what banks call "historical cost accounting." That is, some debt was on their books at its historical cost, or par, although its secondary-market value was far less. Through intricate swaps involving higher-value debt for lower-value debt, the latter could be made to disappear with no loss registered. In this way, some large banks eliminated such countries as Nicaragua and Bolivia from their portfolios while taking on larger amounts of Mexican and Brazilian debts.

Balanced Portfolios

Some banks swapped debt not to reduce or eliminate loans to weak countries but to balance their portfolios. A bank with too much Mexican exposure could exchange it for some other comparable risk, such as Brazil or the Philippines, where its loans were relatively modest. Or a bank might wish to reduce the number of countries in its portfolio to simplify its administration—for example, by exchanging Chilean for Argentine debt. Such transactions could also be structured to avoid any losses—or gains—even though the secondary-market valuations of the loans being exchanged differed.

"Through swapping, banks of one country could exchange debts of other countries for their own country's debt."

In addition, debtor countries swapped loans to alter the foreign-debt exposure of their overseas branches. During the heyday of expanded international lending in the 1970s, many Third World countries entered global capital markets not only as borrowers, but also as lenders. Today this seems absurd, but at the time it was quite fashionable for public and private Latin banks to set up branches in the Bahamas, London, New York, and elsewhere, and to participate in the lending boom side by side with the major multinational banks. Predictably, banks from the larger countries such as Brazil and Mexico were the most numerous and the most active. But Argentine, Colombian, and Venezuelan banks played a significant role, and even Chilean and Peruvian banks dabbled in the Eurodollar market.

When the music stopped in 1982, these Latin banks found themselves in the awkward, not to say farcical, role of holding one another's debts. They were obliged to participate in each other's rescheduling efforts even while claiming hardships of their own. The situation cried out for a remedy.

The remedy was provided by the secondary market. Through swapping, banks of one country could exchange debts of other countries for their own country's debt. Thus Latin banks could shed their foreign loans and end up with what for them were domestic loans. From the debtor countries' point of view, even when carried out by private banks, this process in effect nationalized some of their debt. Although the debt was not retired, it no longer represented the same claim on foreign exchange. All the overseas Latin bank branches have swapped debts this way, and by the end of 1986 most of them will have reduced sharply, if not eliminated, their loans to other countries.

Debt Capitalization

But a market limited to these kinds of swaps would have stagnated at very low levels. Real growth was stimulated when cash buyers appeared. Where did this money come from? It did not come from nontraditional lenders, such as insurance companies or pension funds, which some thought could be lured into the Third World. Having avoided these countries during the boom, these institutions not surprisingly maintained their distance during the bust. Nor did the cash come from private speculators, who have yet to join this drama to any significant degree.

Enter the debtors. For countries, retiring debt through direct purchases at discounted prices was problematical. How could a government plead with banks for lower interest rates and extended maturities while simultaneously prepaying debt through secondary-market purchases? Yet ways were found through imaginative programs of "debt capitalization." In December 1982, Brazil became the first country to adopt a debt capitalization scheme. Chile followed in June 1985 and Mexico announced its own version in mid-1986. Argentina, Bolivia, Costa Rica, and Ecuador are thought to be working on plans. Outside Latin America, the Philippines permitted three deals on an experimental basis and then formulated its program. Nigeria reportedly has also expressed interest. But Latin America is the source of most Third World debt and where most of the debt capitalization remains.

Debt capitalization schemes served two quite

different purposes. One was to stimulate new investment by converting debt to equity. The second was to retire debt. For either purpose, a buyer would purchase foreign debt at a discount and obtain local currency. The debtor country thereby succeeded in retiring some of its foreign debt without using up any scarce foreign exchange.

The basic concept of converting debt to equity is quite simple. It borrows from the process of reorganizing bankrupt corporations with a view to revitalizing them. In corporate reorganizations, a common technique is to convert part of the debt owed to capital stock of the corporation. The result: lower corporate debt and thus lower interest burdens. Lenders receive some stock in the corporation in lieu of their loans, and if the company survives and prospers, they may see some return. The well-publicized Chrysler Corporation bailout scheme employed this technique, and lenders eventually benefited. . . .

Other Options

Debtor countries benefit from these activities since they reduce their debt. But these countries have another option in the secondary market—to purchase their own debt directly. Direct, open purchases by debtor countries were not officially acknowledged as of late 1986, but several have come close. One large Argentine private bank, for instance, purchased substantial amounts of Argentine government debt at discounts and then used that debt to settle its own obligations with multinational banks. This step could only have been taken with Buenos Aires' knowledge and approval. A Venezuelan government bank has been active in purchasing at discounts debt of other Venezuelan government entities. There have been substantial purchases of Peruvian debt under circumstances that suggest governmental involvement, though officially they have been private transactions. This last case is especially interesting, since Peru has been behind on interest payments since October 1984 and since its debt commands only about 22 cents on the dollar. Peru may well have concluded that using, say, $22 million to retire $100 million in debt makes more sense than using this sum at face value to make a small dent in overdue interest, which now exceeds $600 million. It is only a matter of time before this use of the secondary market spreads.

Debt swapping is not a panacea for the debt crisis. Capitalization schemes and direct purchases can chip away at the debt mountain, but these transactions can substantially reduce debt overhang only over a very long period. To begin with, the market is relatively small. The few billion dollars' worth of swaps in 1986 is dwarfed by the several hundred billion dollars or so in total debt of the countries whose debt is traded in the secondary market. Moreover, structural limitations inhibit the use of

the secondary market to retire debt. First, direct foreign investment in Latin America never exceeded more than a few billion dollars annually during the lending boom. Total foreign investment in Mexico, for example, is estimated at only $15 billion, compared with a total debt of some $100 billion. Even if capitalization schemes were to restore the investment flow to earlier levels, these would amount to only a small fraction of the debt service. Second, many of the largest creditors could not bear the financial or the political cost of liquidating their loans at substantial discounts. Therefore, much of the debt probably will not become available on the secondary market.

"The secondary market helps everyone and should be encouraged by regulatory authorities."

Retiring debt through capitalization schemes will be helpful at the margin, but will probably never amount to more than a few per cent per year of a country's debt, if that. Some flight capital may be seduced back (or inhibited from leaving), but political and economic uncertainties will continue to crimp that flow. Direct purchases will also help, but will be constrained by the very foreign-exchange limitations that produced the discounts in the first place.

Implications

The market has a significance beyond its size. As debt swapping expands and develops further, it will profoundly influence debtor-creditor negotiations. Bank creditors simply cannot continue solemnly to negotiate full-interest payments and multi-year reschedulings with debtor governments while dealing in the secondary market for the same debt at substantial discounts. Debtors will point to the market valuations of their loans to legitimate larger concessions, and banks will find it hard to insist on full market terms for rescheduling when the secondary market provides such different signals. . . .

The secondary market helps everyone and should be encouraged by regulatory authorities. Creditors benefit because they can reduce or adjust their portfolios as they see fit. Debtors benefit because they reduce their foreign debt, gaining either an investment or the return of flight capital in the bargain. The financial system is strengthened as banks adjust and as debt burdens are lowered. Banks must continue to build their loan loss reserves but should not be required to register specific losses as a result of swapping debt.

Although swapping per se is no panacea for the debt crisis, the secondary market does contain the seeds of a more profound solution. As numerous analysts have suggested, the most promising approach to easing the crisis involves a partial assumption of the debt by public-sector entities in exchange for substantial interest-rate relief. The secondary market both suggests the basis for doing this and provides a mechanism. The basis would be to use the secondary-market valuation to determine the amount of interest-rate relief provided. The mechanism would be a swap: government bonds for Third World debt.

Suppose some public entity—the World Bank, developed-country governments, or some combination of the two—offered to swap its bonds for debts of troubled debtors. The swap would be voluntary and would be conditioned on a range of economic and political reforms. Obviously, the interest rate on these bonds would be lower than the rates on the debt, and the savings could be passed on to the debtor countries.

A Fair Trade

The main problems would involve determining the savings and avoiding offering relief to stronger countries. A solution could be based on the market valuation of a given country's debt. For example, Brazil's debt is offered at around 75 per cent of face value. In today's market, a government-entity 15-year dollar bond with an interest rate of 4.9 per cent would have a similar price. Mexico's debt goes for roughly 57 per cent of face value—approximately equivalent to a government-entity 15-year bond with an interest rate of 2.75 per cent. Hence, the government entity could issue bonds with those interest rates and offer to swap them on a one-for-one basis with banks. It would offer the 4.9 per cent bonds for Brazilian debt and the 2.75 per cent bonds for Mexican debt.

"Swapping would contribute to raising living standards in both debtor and creditor countries."

The rate on the government bonds, then, would depend on the value of the specific country debt for which they are swapped. This policy preserves differences among countries and concentrates assistance where it is needed most. Relatively well-off countries whose debt sells for relatively higher prices in the secondary market would receive bonds with correspondingly higher interest rates. A country whose debt commanded a very low market price would receive bonds with lower interest rates, and possibly longer maturities, to equalize their value with the value of that country's debts in the secondary market.

Debt swapping on this grand scale would not be a substitute for the economic and political reforms needed in debtor countries. On the contrary, only reforming debtor countries would be eligible to participate. Thus large-scale debt swapping would overcome a fatal weakness of the Baker plan—its insufficient incentives to carry out economic change that could be painful in the short run.

Moreover, this approach provides incentives in the right proportions. The least solvent countries probably need the most thoroughgoing reforms, and will have the greatest difficulty adopting them. They therefore need the strongest incentives. This form of debt swapping provides them through lower interest rates on bonds. Economically healthier countries would qualify for and receive less interest-rate relief through the bond swap.

Banks that accepted this swap would suffer reduced interest income in future years, but they would also strengthen their balance sheets by replacing uncertain assets with riskless ones. Regulators should facilitate the swap by not requiring any write-down, permitting banks to swap if they wished with no immediate effect on their balance sheets. Passing on the interest savings to debtors would strengthen the banks' financial situation and make repayment more likely. And because repayment would be more likely, there should be no cost to the bond-issuing government entity, which would be able to collect enough from Brazil and Mexico to make the necessary payments on the bonds it had issued.

Mutual Benefits

The broader political and economic gains would probably exceed the financial gains. Such swapping could defuse a smoldering crisis. It could avert a political confrontation that threatens to sour relations between the United States and many Third World countries. In fact, it would enable the United States to exercise leadership to alleviate severe financial strains in a way that would benefit all concerned. The resulting improvements for both debtors and creditors would facilitate economic growth worldwide and would increase trade—which would mean greater purchases of U.S. goods. Therefore, swapping would contribute to raising living standards in both debtor and creditor countries. Finally, this approach is consistent with free markets, whose emergence and valuation provide its very framework.

Richard S. Weinert is president of Leslie, Weinert and Company, a New York investment banking firm.

The US Should Not Threaten Protectionist Measures

Lawrence J. Lau

The United States is the world's largest trading nation. It has also been the world's staunchest supporter of the principle of free trade in the postwar period. From the original creation of the General Agreement on Tariffs and Trade (GATT), immediately after World War II, through the Kennedy and Tokyo Rounds of multilateral tariff reductions of the 1960s and 1970s up to the latest Uruguay Round of trade negotiations, the United States has consistently been pressing for the liberalization of the worldwide exchange of goods and services.

The United States supports free trade on the grounds that voluntary exchange of goods and services always raises the welfare of all trading partners, permits the international specialization of production according to the principle of comparative advantage, and leads to the highest and best use of scarce resources for all. However, the series of unprecedented large trade deficits since 1984 has roused widespread protectionist sentiments in the United States. . . .

Many people in the United States became alarmed by the sheer magnitude as well as the suddenness of the increase in the real trade deficit. Some attributed the slowdown in the growth rate of the real GNP [gross national product] of the United States since 1984 (compared with the immediately preceding two-year period) to the large trade deficit. Some were concerned that the large trade deficit indicated that as a nation the United States expended far more—on consumption, investment, and government expenditures—than it produced and that this situation could not continue indefinitely. Some took the large trade deficit as another sign of declining competitiveness of U.S. exports in the world market.

Others interpreted the large trade deficit as yet further evidence of unfair trading practices of our trading partners.

As the large trade deficit was brought about by rapidly rising real imports and almost stagnant real exports, many domestic industries were adversely affected because of sales lost to and replaced by imports. Some domestic industries also suffered because of their inability to expand exports. For these "injured" industries, profits fell and jobs were lost.

Against this background, many industries and workers demand relief in the form of protection, that is, a government policy aimed at restricting imports at either the aggregate or the industry level.

However, the large increases in the U.S. trade deficit since 1984 were distributed fairly uniformly among its trading partners and product groups. The bilateral real trade deficit position of the United States widened with almost every major trading partner to approximately the same degree. Likewise the real trade deficit position of almost every product group also widened to more or less the same degree. Thus, no single trading partner or product group can be singled out as the primary cause of the large trade deficit.

What a Trade Deficit Means

The first thing to realize about trade surpluses and deficits is that it is impossible for all countries to run surpluses (or, for that matter, deficits) *at the same time.* Unless every country's trade surplus or deficit is exactly zero, there will always be at least one country running a trade surplus and one running a deficit. Moreover, the trade deficit (or surplus) is exactly equal to the difference between real gross national expenditure (GNE)—defined as the sum of real private domestic consumption, real gross domestic investment, and real total (federal, state, and local) government expenditures—and real

Lawrence J. Lau, "Trade and Protectionism: What Should Be Done?" *The World & I*, May 1987.

GNP. If real GNE exceeds real GNP, the nation as a whole is spending more than it currently produces, and the difference is made up by real net imports, or equivalently the real trade deficit. If real GNP exceeds real GNE, the nation is spending less than it currently produces, and the difference is the real trade surplus. Thus, trade surpluses and trade deficits are reflections of whether a nation currently uses more or less resources than its current output.

"There is really nothing intrinsically good or bad about a trade surplus or deficit."

One useful way to look at the trade deficit is that it represents a loan from the surplus country, which is deferring current use of part of its output, to the deficit country, which is enjoying immediate use of additional resources over and above its own output. In the process, the surplus country accumulates claims in the form of currency, bonds, or other obligations of the deficit country. At some future time, the surplus country can use these assets for the purchase of imports from the deficit country in excess of its future exports to the deficit country. When that occurs, the once-deficit country will run a trade surplus and will be spending less than it produces. The once-surplus country will run a deficit and will be able to enjoy the use of resources greater than its output. Thus, trade surpluses and deficits may essentially be regarded as the outcomes of borrowing and lending among nations. The ability to borrow and lend enhances the welfare of nations just as much as it does the welfare of individual households, resulting in greater efficiency in the intertemporal allocation of resources. It is worth noting that a country will run a trade deficit both when it is borrowing and when it is being repaid.

Two Conditions

A trade deficit is possible only if two conditions are simultaneously met—first, the nation as a whole desires to expend more then it currently produces, and second, the trading partner countries are willing to lend their resources (through either loans, direct investments, or portfolio investments) to the deficit country. If desired real GNE is less than or equal to real GNP, there cannot be a trade defict. Similarly, if trading partner countries are unwilling to lend to the deficit country, a trade deficit is also impossible.

Historically, the United States was a net borrower during most of the nineteenth century, incurring substantial trade deficits that provided the extra resources for its development. In the immediate post-World War II period, the United States was a net lender and helped finance much of the postwar reconstruction of Western Europe and Japan. In the late 1960s and early 1970s, the direction of capital flow reversed, and the United States ran a string of trade deficits. Between 1980 and 1982, the United States once again had record surpluses. But then the trade balance turned into a deficit in 1983 and grew to $150 billion in 1986. . . .

Neutral Value of a Deficit

On the trade deficit itself, there is really nothing intrinsically good or bad about a trade surplus or deficit. It is simply the outcome of the balance of market forces: our demand for imports, foreigners' demand for our exports, and foreigners' net demand for U.S. assets. One cannot say whether a trade balance of zero is better than a trade deficit. Moreover, if the United States were somehow in a deep recession, the real aggregate demand would fall so much that the country would most certainly have a trade surplus, but that would hardly be a desirable outcome.

However, some of us who are more farsighted may worry about borrowing too much from abroad. After all, all borrowings have to be repaid eventually. This is a legitimate concern because when the time of repayment arrives we shall have to make do with less than our output at the time, which may lower our living standard. This means that the manner in which we use the borrowed resources may make a difference. For example, if all of the borrowed resources were used to finance increases in private consumption and not investment, future outputs may not grow fast enough to maintain our living standard at the time of repayment. Fortunately, part of the borrowed resources, equivalent to approximately 2 percent of real GNP, was used to finance additional investment. This investment will raise future output more than if it were not made and hence will provide the margin for the repayment to our trading partners.

Thus, at the macroeconomic level there seems to be little reason to worry about the trade deficit per se. However, at the industry level, there are problems caused by the rapid increase in total imports and stagnancy in exports. Specifically, industries (both exporting and importing) may be "injured" by the competition of foreign goods both in the United States and in foreign markets, resulting in lost profits and jobs. In addition, the rapidity of the increase in imports makes it diffcult for firms and workers to adjust to the new circumstances. One should, however, try to distinguish between the problem of the trade deficit and the problem of "injured" industries. Even if there were no trade deficit or, for that matter, a trade surplus, as long as there are imports, there will be industries that will claim to be "injured." Relative expansion of some industries and relative contraction of others are the inevitable results of international specialization made possible by trade.

The problem of "injured" industries is actually a more general problem of declining industries. Firms and workers may also become dislocated from internal domestic competition and technological change. In all of these instances, if it can be established that the causes of the decline were permanent—for example, the exhaustion of a mineral resource—the best thing that a government can do is to facilitate the redeployment of the workers and other resources as quickly as possible and to minimize their transitional pain, not try to prop up these industries indefinitely.

Determining whether a decline is permanent is not so easy. However, if firms and workers genuinely believe that the decline is only temporary, they should request, and the government should provide, only temporary short-term relief, and they should be prepared to demonstrate their confidence in the future of the industry by making needed new investments and deferring part of the current wages.

> *"Even if there were no trade deficit, . . . as long as there are imports, there will be industries that will claim to be 'injured.'"*

For industries whose declines were caused by foreign competition, there is an additional complicating factor because whether the decline is permanent depends also on the expectations of the future movements of the exchange rate. Firms that were "injured" by imports in the last few years may now find themselves competitive once again under current exchange rates. In any case, the volatility of the exchange rate—a swing of up to 80 percent against some major currencies in five years—poses problems of both short-term and long-term adjustments not only to the United States but also to its trading partners.

Solutions

The first thing that can be done is to try to increase exports (even though this may not do anything for industries "injured" by imports). Under the present circumstances, a coordinated expansion by the other industrialized countries and a satisfactory resolution of the Latin American debt problem will create increased demand for U.S. exports.

Second, such demand will be additionally stimulated by the considerable decline of the U.S. exchange rate since early 1985. In the long term, the objective should be to secure a stable exchange rate in an open and orderly market and to moderate the big swings in relative currency values.

Third, one can adopt what may be called "market opening" measures. Our trading partners should be persuaded to lower formal and informal barriers to trade in goods and services. . . . Free trade areas with selected trading partners are another possibility.

Fourth, one can intensify the enforcement of fair trade practices, including antidumping statutes and infringements of patents, copyrights, and trade secrets.

Fifth, one can promote and support research and development so as to maintain our lead in technology and improve our productivity, accelerate the spin-off of defense-related research for civilian use and facilitate the export of high-technology products by streamlining the control procedures.

Sixth, one can provide assistance to firms and workers, especially the latter, in dislocated industries so that they can become profitably employed in other industries. The most important measure is the provision of funds for the retraining, placement, and relocation of dislocated workers.

Seventh, one can provide temporary relief to industries that are temporarily "injured" by imposing temporary protection. This may take the form of tariffs and quotas, for example, against sudden surges of imports in specific industries. This authority is sometimes referred to as Section 201 authority. It is assumed, however, that the "injured" industry can in fact recover eventually, at which time the protection can be withdrawn.

Finally, there is permanent protection, that is, either tariffs or quotas are imposed on products to limit their entry into the United States indefinitely. Many "temporarily protected" products become defacto permanently protected. Examples include textiles and apparel, sugar, steel, and automobiles.

Costs of Protection

Protection is costly to the economy and society in many ways. Unfortunately, the costs are frequently invisible because their burdens are widely dispersed over the society at large. Any form of protectionism, be it tariffs or quotas, always raises prices. Not only will the prices of imports increase, but the prices of import-substituting products and the products previously using imports as inputs will also increase. One study suggests that as a result of protection, the retail prices of protected products are on average 10 percent higher than otherwise. The total cost to American consumers of existing protection has been estimated by Gary C. Hufbauer of the Institute for International Economics at $65 billion in 1986, or more than $250 per person per year.

Protection results in additional costs to the economy if resources (capital and labor) continue to be used in declining industries instead of being redeployed to other industries where they can be applied more efficiently. Thus both investment and labor flows are distorted by protection.

Finally, protection, once instituted, is extremely difficult to eliminate, and this effectively removes any further incentive for the protected industry to be efficient, further adding to the costs borne by society.

There is no doubt that protectionist measures will decrease imports. However, given the possibility of retaliation, it is not at all clear whether protectionist measures, when implemented and retaliated against, will actually narrow the trade deficit or will actually increase the total number of jobs in the whole economy. What is certain is that protectionist measures will increase prices and reduce aggregate real output and welfare.

In the short run, protectionist measures may be justified as a means of reducing disruption of industries and workers. However, permanent protection of industries has little economic merit.

Moreover, permanent protection of some industries tends to encourage other industries to seek similar permanent protection themselves rather than improve their productivity through cost-cutting and technological innovation. If permanent protection becomes widespread, we shall have a stagnant and inefficient economy with little innovation in the long run.

"Protectionism is not a solution to the problem of the large trade deficit."

Moreover, in view of the fact that the real value of the U.S. dollar has by now already declined more than 20 percent from its peak, many U.S. exports are competitive again. The real trade deficit is already narrowing as of the last quarter of 1986, albeit slowly. Some critics may argue that the adjustment is too slow. However, we should bear in mind that a lag of two years in the adjustment of imports or exports to changes in the exchange rate is not unusual. For example, even though the U.S. exchange rate rose steeply in late 1980 and was more than 30 percent higher by the end of 1983, the United States continued to run a significant trade surplus in 1982 and only a relatively small trade deficit in 1983.

Say No to Protectionism

If it were true that the market is finally turning in favor of our exports and against our imports, it would seem unwise to impose protectionist measures now to slow down imports that would have slowed anyway and invite retaliation by our trading partners against our exports, which are poised to grow. So even if one considers protectionism desirable, this is not the right time to implement it.

One must conclude that protectionism is not a solution to the problem of the large trade deficit, except as a temporary instrument to reduce

disruption of "injured" industries while they undergo orderly long-term adjustments. It is also not a satisfactory solution for industries in long-term decline. Coordination of economic policies with the major industrialized countries, stabilization of the exchange rate, market opening, intensified enforcement of fair trade practices, increased support of research and development, and worker retraining and relocation will help. All of these measures have been either undertaken or proposed by the U.S. government or are in the various pending trade bills in Congress. They deserve to be supported.

Lawrence J. Lau is a professor of economics at Stanford University.

The US Should Threaten Protectionist Measures

Howard Banks

Get ready for yet more depressing trade numbers, no matter how low the dollar falls. The U.S. merchandise trade deficit will improve by much less in 1987 than was hoped. At best, last year's $170 billion deficit will decline by no more than $10 billion to $20 billion. The figures will be better in 1988—sufficiently so to produce an economic pickup—but still leaving a trade gap that is simply not sustainable.

This is the consensus view of half a dozen major international forecasting groups that gathered privately in Washington in mid-January [1987]. Consensus is often wrong, of course, especially in economic matters, but the essential point remains: Even if the dollar goes substantially lower, the U.S. seems doomed to run a huge deficit in its balance of merchandise trade as far out as the eye can see.

The public is hardened to horrifyingly big numbers, and none of this might lead to political action for a long time if it weren't costing jobs in sensitive industries—a topic certain to grab any politician right where it hurts. "It [trade] is absolutely the number one issue," says Senate Finance Committee Chairman Lloyd Bentsen (D-Tex.), who will lead the political charge for protectionism in this session of Congress. "We need a tough, coordinated trade policy." Trade policy is, of course, a euphemism for protectionism.

Such statements make the blood run cold in the veins of free traders or those who believe that market forces, left to work their ways, will eventually bring trade back into balance. Whether the market alone could solve the problem in the long run is academic. In the long run, to paraphrase Lord Keynes, the politicians would all be defeated.

Why abandon the principles of free trade, which have served the world so well for the past 40 years? The answer is that free trade has been practiced, chiefly by the U.S., in the real sense of throwing its borders wide open to anyone who has anything to sell. Today's problems didn't just happen. They are the consequence of American willingness to open its borders to foreign goods even though elsewhere free trade has been modified to suit the imagined or real economic interests of individual nations.

Bluntly put, we have permitted foreign countries to use freely their advantages of lower wage rates, lower defense-spending burdens and domestic subsidies to bite off huge pieces of the U.S. market. They, in turn, have thrown up barriers to exercise by the U.S. of many of our natural advantages, such as our low-cost agriculture and advanced technology. We freely permit the import of Brazilian shoes, while the Brazilians keep U.S. small computers out of their market. We have ceded our consumer electronics market to the Japanese and other Asian countries, while they keep for themselves markets like defense and high technology.

The wonder is it took so long for the situation to reach crisis point.

The Most Practical Trade Weapon

How much help will the cheaper dollar be in checking the crisis? A fair amount. The betting is the Fed will soon cut interest rates again and, maybe, pump out more money. Hence the continued weakness in the dollar vis-á-vis the mark and the yen. Devaluation is, after all, the most practical trade weapon the U.S. has readily available. It requires no legislation, no painful negotiations and makes retaliation difficult. The cheaper dollar encourages foreigners to buy U.S. goods and services, makes imported goods dearer in the U.S.

But there are limits to devaluation. . . .

Paul Krugman, an MIT economics professor and editor of an excellent book, *Strategic Trade Policy and*

Howard Banks, "No More Mr. Nice Guy." Excerpted by permission of *Forbes* magazine, February 9, 1987. © Forbes Inc., 1987.

the New International Economics, says: "This is one of those rare times when the U.S. can reduce its trade problems by printing money."

But Krugman dashes cold water on those who think that changes in exchange rates alone can close the trade gap to bearable dimensions: "No one sensible would say that the U.S. can restore its competitive position [solely] via the printing press. That would lead to overheating and eventually resumed inflation."

Force Down the Dollar

Still, forcing down the dollar seems the handiest weapon right now. It will help bludgeon the Germans and the Japanese, in particular, to stimulate their economies. This would relieve some of the pressure on the U.S. market, divert some goods that are now coming here to the German and Japanese markets, and would stimulate the demand for U.S. goods abroad.

In recent years, selling to the U.S. has been just about the only thing going for the world economy. "In the 1982 through 1985 period, the U.S. absorbed 55% of the increase in non-oil LDC [less developed country] exports, while Japan took just 10% of the extra and the European Economic Community 20%," says Robert Strauss, the most effective trade representative the U.S. has ever seen (he was U.S. trade ambassador in the Carter Administration). A look at the numbers shows how exclusively the U.S. has borne the burden of keeping world trade flowing. Today the U.S. buys 55% of the manufactured goods exported by the developing countries, while Western Europe takes half that much and Japan a measly 9%. Expanding their shares to the same per capita level as the U.S. would add an estimated $250 billion a year to world trade.

"A pure market solution—depending on new exchange parities—would not close the gap sufficiently and fast enough."

Yet, for all their pious talk about helping the poorer countries, Germany and Japan refuse to play their part. Japan reneged on earlier promises that it would get its economy growing again and then introduced its most austere budget since 1955. It did increase defense spending, to just over 1% of GNP, but will extra business go to U.S. suppliers? No, to Mitsubishi, even though its cost of building aircraft in Japan is simply outrageous. Why not buy American armaments, thus improving the balance of payments situation? National interest—or perceived national interest.

The Germans remain haughtily aloof.... The theory is that if their currencies rapidly appreciate

against the dollar, they will have little choice but to lower interest rates and get their economy growing. Either that, or their economies sink from today's stagnation into deep recession.

But even if we get some help from Germany and Japan and from a weaker dollar, don't forget that half of U.S. trade now is with countries like Canada or Australia whose currencies haven't gone down against the dollar. Or with countries like South Korea that, for obviously sensible reasons from their point of view, peg their currencies to the dollar.

Trade Surplus

A major problem, and one that won't yield readily to the devaluation cure, involves the so-called structural elements to the overseas trade surplus—meaning trade flows that are built into the system. Take Japanese investment in the U.S. The 2-million-car-a-year Japanese-owned capacity that will be in place by 1990 may provide U.S. jobs, but it will suck in steady flows of Japanese components and machine tools and engineering consultancy and the rest—since they come from suppliers the owners know and trust. And, significantly, U.S.-controlled multinational companies are themselves a part of the problem.

The simple truth is this: A pure market solution—depending on new exchange parities—would not close the gap sufficiently and fast enough to satisfy the voters. Or the politicians, come to that; hence the push for protectionism, which they believe will cut the trade deficit. "But the two are separate. Trade policy is a micro issue, the deficit is a macro one. Politicians don't understand the distinction," says Fred Bergsten, director of the Institute for International Economics. The root cause of the trade deficit is the budget deficit, but neither White House nor Congress shows any stomach to tackle that.

The push is being led by what is called the Texas mafia, whose voice is said to have long dominated matters of trade. Today's ranking members: Senate Finance Committee Chairman Lloyd Bentsen (D-Tex.), Treasury Secretary James Baker III, House Majority Leader Jim Wright (D-Tex.), Representative Bill Archer (R-Tex.), and Bob Strauss.

What forms would U.S. protectionism take?

Some of what will be proposed will be what Harald Malmgren, president of Malmgren, Inc. and former trade negotiator in the Carter Administration, calls technical protection. This will include tightening the timetables on dumping and countervailing duty cases, and also limiting presidential discretion to sidestep cases for foreign policy reasons, despite complaints from the State Department.

Moreover, for better or worse, the Reagan Administration is becoming less doctrinaire in its support for free trade and is more willing than in the past to sacrifice foreign policy to domestic economic interests.

This change to an active stance on trade from the White House can be most clearly seen in the increasing number of so-called gray actions, like voluntary restraint agreements, used to redress trade grievances. There have been new deals to help U.S. machine tools and lumber. The chips deal with the Japanese, however, is so out of kilter with the marketplace that it is collapsing under its own weight. (This restraint also offends U.S. computer makers who want cheap chips, even if they are dumped, so as to stay competitive themselves—a typical trade policy conflict. Look for similar conflicts as many U.S. retailers face loss of their supplies of cheap foreign goods.)

"The rest of the world must understand that the present [trade] situation cannot continue. So, it's no more Mr. Nice Guy."

The U.S. is increasingly frustrated by the ineffectiveness of the General Agreement on Tariffs & Trade. The treaty now covers just 5% or so of world trade, vs. 20% in 1950. Getting an answer from GATT to a problem "is like dropping a rose petal over the Grand Canyon and waiting for the echo," complains Senator Bentsen. And U.S. Trade Representative Clayton Yeutter is hanging tough in the talks leading to the new round of GATT talks. "Yes," he says, "we're going to be recalcitrant until we get the issues resolved in the right way in Geneva."...

The U.S. is keen to open the telecommunications market worldwide but has just been slapped in the face by the French. They are blocking AT&T from buying more than a 20% stake (it wanted 60%) in CGCT, the moneylosing telecommunications group that was appropriated from ITT by the Mitterrand government. The Germans are said to have encouraged the French to limit competition in Europe. Meanwhile, and no surprise to anyone, the Japanese are hedging on opening their telecommunications market.

Our trading partners have been able to impose this double standard because the U.S. has failed to convince them that we will retaliate. Too much Mr. Nice Guy.

Import Surcharge

Next year, 1988, is a presidential election year. The pressure to "do something" about trade will be at the boiling point. One extreme possibility would be an across-the-board import surcharge of, say, 10%—or roughly $40 billion a year. It would be a tax increase on consumption, by another name, and could be applied to help bring down the budget deficit. It would also be likely to slow—or stop—the economy. But it would be permitted under GATT, because it would be applied for balance-of-payments reasons. In fact, it's just the prescription routinely proposed by the International Monetary Fund for less-developed countries in trouble.

Expect to hear such bizarre-sounding proposals as an official auction market for the import quotas. If it is determined, say, that 2 million Japanese cars should be allowed into the U.S. each year, Japanese carmakers would be allowed to bid for quotas. This would transfer to the U.S. some of the higher profits importers make when there are quotas—look what happened with Japanese cars, or steel—at the expense of higher consumer prices here. Such money could pay for retraining or relocating workers displaced by imports.

Will the U.S. go this far? Will it impose an auction system or an across-the-board import surtax? Only as a last resort. But the threat is real.

Where is all this leading us? The world economy and trading system is at a watershed of a sort not experienced since the Marshall Plan rescued the industrial economies from the ravages of World War II. The 40-year mix of mostly magnanimous economic policies here helped develop the rapid growth in world trade to $2 trillion a year. But now the assumptions on which U.S. trade policy has been based have been overtaken by events. In the U.S. merchandise imports were 4.1% of GNP in 1960; in 1985 they were 10.2% and rising.

The situation is complicated for the U.S. because, without a gold standard, our dollar is now the world's sole reserve currency. Oil is priced in dollars, investments flow in dollars, nations hold their reserves in dollars. The volume of financial transactions is now roughly 25 times the volume of total world trade.

The Breaking Point

These fundamental shifts have stretched U.S. resources to the breaking point. This country is no longer rich enough to carry world trade and Free World defense unaided. In simplistic terms, Uncle Sam is mad, and he isn't going to take it any longer.

Consumer groups will cry over the reductions in availability of some cheap goods. Foreign governments will lecture us on our selfishness and lack of responsibility. But, remember: The only reason that countries like Germany, Japan, Taiwan, South Korea and the rest are as well off as they are is because of near free access to the U.S. market. Now they are going to have to pay something for that. That means: Revalue their currencies and reflate domestic demand to take the heat off the U.S. economy.

The Europeans and the Japanese especially can pay much more for their own defense. The Japanese say, "That would mean we'd have to adopt nuclear weapons," as though that's supposed to kill the debate. Maybe it's time to tell 'em to go ahead.

There will be screams from the banks about their LDC debt. But how far can we sacrifice U.S. industry to save the banks from huge writeoffs?

And there'll be screams that the U.S.' hanging tough might risk South Korea, the Philippines, Brazil going communist. It's unlikely they would be that foolish; the world trend is in fact toward democracy. Take a chance.

Will all of this lead to a terrible trade war in which everybody suffers and developing countries default on their debt, and democracy is set back? Will the dollar go deep into the tank?

Probably not—although the air will turn blue with threats and confrontations. The problem will gradually yield, not to one but to several approaches. There will be more bilateral trade demands made by the U.S.: We'll buy your shoes only if you permit us to sell personal computers. You want to sell us cars? Then open your markets to American citrus fruits and American wheat.

The cheaper dollar, too, will make a big difference, especially as it spreads to exchange against currencies other than the yen and the mark.

Pay Attention to Trade

The State Department will begin paying less attention to diplomacy and more attention to trade. "We must give up the outdated illusion of being the world's political and industrial leader. Acting as if we still are can only destroy us," says Andrew Grove, president and chief executive of chipmaker Intel Corp.

However reluctantly, Germany and Japan, and other countries, will begin to stimulate their economies.

All these things are likely to happen, not because the U.S. will turn aggressively protectionist, but because the possibility of its doing so would have consequences too horrible to contemplate. But the rest of the world must understand that the present situation cannot continue. So, it's no more Mr. Nice Guy—and our trading partners better believe it.

Howard Banks writes for Forbes, *a business and finance magazine.*

"America did not grow strong by erecting trade barriers and reneging on international obligations."

Free Trade Would Solve the Trade Deficit

Clayton Yeutter

The United States is the world's most important trading nation. Some five million American jobs depend upon exports and the days when the U.S. could build a wall around itself and ignore foreign trade are over—if they ever existed at all. Once, in the early 1930s, this nation did attempt to withdraw from the world by erecting mammoth trade barriers and in so doing contributed to and prolonged a disastrous worldwide depression. But after World War II, all major trading nations joined together to create a new international trade system built on the principle of trade liberalization.

The expansion of world trade in the 40 years since then has spawned growing prosperity, not only here at home, but also around the world. As the world's trading nations grew more interdependent, we have prospered together. In the last 25 years, world trade has grown five-fold, helping to boost the world's gross national product in real terms from $5.3 trillion to $14 trillion. This phenomenon was not limited to the developed nations. The developing world saw its GNP growth rate keep step with that of the industrial nations.

Yet, for all its success, the international trade system faces serious problems. A breakdown in discipline has led to rising trade barriers around the world. Here at home, patience has worn thin as our trade deficit has risen to more than $170 billion per year.

President Reagan began his second term determined to address our growing trade problem, not by cutting us off from the world and hurting workers whose jobs depend on exports, but by addressing the root causes of our trade deficit. I joined the Administration at that time to help the President in this effort.

During the summer of 1985, we reevaluated U.S. trade policy in dozens of cabinet and sub-cabinet meetings. We met with representatives of the private sector, with members of Congress, and with policy experts. All this rethinking culminated in a major address in September 1985 in which President Reagan announced an aggressive, non-protectionist trade strategy that addressed the real causes of our trade imbalance. That strategy has brought marked success.

We stepped up our efforts to eliminate other nations' unfair trade practices and achieved numerous significant market-opening results. We redoubled our efforts to improve international trade rules and achieved an agreement to launch the Uruguay Round of multilateral trade negotiations. And we attacked fundamental international economic problems and achieved a substantial improvement in what had been an overvalued dollar.

Unfair Trade Practices

The first part of the President's trade strategy is to fight unfair trade practices of other countries. Too often in the past, we overlooked transgressions by other countries in the belief that, because of our strong economy, we could afford to be magnanimous. But with a huge trade deficit of our own, we are now insisting that our trading partners fulfill their obligation to play by the rules of the international trade system.

President Reagan is implementing the laws governing unfair trade practices more aggressively than the U.S. has ever done. Last fall [1986], for example, he brought unfair trade cases against several trading partners—the first time any President had self-initiated cases under Section 301 of the Trade Act.

Since then, we have achieved impressive results, reversing unfair foreign practices involving trade in agriculture, high technology and services. . . .

Clayton Yeutter, "Protectionism," a speech delivered to the Foreign Trade Association of Southern California on January 29, 1987.

We were able to achieve a precedent-setting agreement with Korea when we convinced that country to open its market to foreign insurance firms. It was our first unfair trade practice case involving a service industry, and it has turned out quite well.

In another major case with another major trading partner, we successfully negotiated an agreement with Canada that will neutralize what we deem to be unfair subsidies on softwood lumber entering the American market. This will save thousands of jobs in the U.S. timber industry and enable many sawmills here on the West Coast to remain open.

We also achieved important access in the Japanese, Korean and Taiwanese markets for American cigarette manufacturers. These agreements could generate hundreds of millions—and possibly billions—of dollars in new sales for American cigarette exporters.

"The United States is now on the verge of turning around the trade problem."

In a couple of other victories for American agribusiness, we successfully challenged European subsidies for canned fruit processing and got the European Community (EC) to offset its Mediterranean preferences for citrus imports by granting additional access to its market for U.S. citrus producers. As a side-benefit to the citrus settlement, we also obtained significantly lower tariffs on our almond exports to the EC—an important breakthrough for almond growers in California. . . .

Fix the System

The second element of the President's trade strategy is to fix the international trade system, a system that simply is not working properly.

As an institution, GATT [General Agreement on Tariffs and Trade] has arguably done more over the past 40 years to promote the cause of peace and prosperity than any other international body. Yet, like all institutions, GATT must change with the times or run the risk of becoming obsolete. As currently constituted, GATT does not address the realities of modern trade.

Many countries are closing their doors to imports because they believe they can skirt or circumvent the rules that govern world trade. However, the way to fix the system is not to break the rules ourselves, as some protectionists would argue, but to make GATT itself stronger and more effective.

President Reagan is the leading advocate of a new worldwide GATT negotiation to improve international trading rules. His persistence paid off

last September [1986] when ministers from the 92 GATT nations agreed in Punta del Este, Uruguay to launch a new round of multilateral negotiations. This decision was a major victory for free and fair trade. It offers hope to workers and farmers burdened by the inadequacies of the existing world trade system. . . .

Encourage US Exports

The third element of the President's trade policy is perhaps the most important: changing global economic policies that discourage U.S. exports and place our import-sensitive industries at a significant competitive advantage.

During the President's first term, our economic growth was much higher than that of most other countries, leading to a strengthening of the dollar, which in turn made it difficult for U.S. exporters to sell on the world market. The strong dollar also made imports comparatively cheap, which increased the economic stress on U.S. industries such as steel, textiles, and footwear.

We should not and will not change the policies that have created strong economic growth at home, even though they may secondarily increase the value of the dollar. It is only through economic growth that we create jobs and boost our standard of living. But we are encouraging other nations—not only in Western Europe and Japan but less developed countries (LDCs) as well—to emulate our economic success and improve their own rates of economic growth. A narrowing of the growth gap will begin to correct the economic disequilibrium that has so distorted trade flows.

We in the U.S. must also help by dramatically reducing our own federal budget deficit. By spending and borrowing less, our government would free up funds for private sector investment and reduce our dependence upon foreign capital.

We have already made some progress on this front. Most of the macroeconomic policy changes I've just mentioned were agreed to by participants at the Tokyo Economic Summit. In addition, at its annual meeting in Seoul, the International Monetary Fund accepted Secretary Baker's proposition that the LDCs need to grow their way out of debt, thereby increasing imports as well as exports. Subsequent IMF-World Bank meetings in Washington endorsed many of these basic concepts, though not with unanimity. And at home, the budget deficit is finally beginning to shrink—this year [1987] it could decline by $30-$40 billion, and next year should bring a comparable improvement.

Declining Dollar

In the past year [1986], the value of the dollar has declined significantly against the yen and the major European currencies. This is now beginning to put American exporters back in business. U.S. products and services that once were too costly because of the strong dollar are becoming competitive in foreign markets. That should help our import-sensitive industries, too, as cheap imports become not-so-cheap.

Unfortunately, this exchange rate adjustment has not affected all currencies equally. The Canadian dollar and many of the currencies of the Far East and Latin America have not strengthened against the dollar. Because a great deal of our trading volume is with those countries, we face continued trade deficits until we experience dollar adjustments against those currencies too.

Even where we have seen a major change in the dollar against other currencies, it will take time for this adjustment to be reflected in the trade deficit numbers. Businessmen simply don't change buying patterns overnight. Moreover, not all of the exchange rate effect has been passed through in the form of price increases, since many foreign exporters accept a squeezing of profits in order to maintain market share.

The so-called J-curve effect has caused the trade deficit to widen in the short run as domestic buyers temporarily continue to purchase imports at higher prices. But as order books begin to reflect the new exchange-rate realities, imports should fall while exports begin to pick up. The change may not be as quick as we would like, for we simply cannot reverse a five-year phenomenon in a short period. But our policy direction is sound and improvement is on the way.

The United States is now on the verge of turning around the trade problem. We are achieving many long-sought objectives. We have torn down trade barriers in other countries. We have launched a new round of GATT negotiations. And we have seen the dollar readjust against other major currencies. Wouldn't it be a shame if we reversed this progress by passing protectionist legislation?

Yet last year [1986] many in Congress seemed determined to propose protectionist measures. Those bills would not have brought fair trade; they would only have brought less trade—to the detriment of us all. That would be the worst of all worlds. We'd cause global trading volumes to shrink just as we're becoming more competitive.

Reject Protectionism

Although we will continue to reject thinly-veiled protectionist measures, the Administration is willing to work with responsible members of Congress on constructive legislation. In his State of the Union message, President Reagan established a national goal of assuring American competitive preeminence into the 21st century. His comprehensive plan to achieve this goal includes modifications in our trade law to improve our international competitiveness.

For example, we will support additional funding

for a "war chest" to match export credits offered by our competitors. $100 million was appropriated for this purpose. The President has also requested authority to negotiate the new GATT round on a fast-track basis. And he has proposed a number of changes in our trade laws designed to make it easier to go after other nations' unfair trade practices.

President Reagan also believes our laws should be strengthened to provide better protection for American intellectual property. And our anti-trust laws should be reformed to make American companies more competitive in the international marketplace.

These and other proposals that the Administration is prepared to endorse would enhance U.S. exporting opportunities, not diminish them. They are positive, forward-looking, aggressive. They reflect President Reagan's confidence in America and its people, the antithesis of the defeatism that is reflected in protectionist legislation. U.S. protectionism would certainly torpedo the new GATT round and launch a dangerous spiral of retaliation and counter-retaliation.

"Expanding trade opportunities will bring higher living standards for all."

The big losers in a trade war would be farmers and the workers of our most dynamic industries who would find overseas markets closed to them, and American consumers who would pay higher prices on thousands of products. The U.S. would lose jobs in our most competitive areas—in the aircraft, business machines, high tech, paper, chemical, agricultural and other machinery and food processing industries. Farmers would lose export sales. . . .

It seems senseless to punish workers in our most efficient industries or to jeopardize the livelihood of the five million Americans whose jobs depend upon exports.

America did not grow strong by erecting trade barriers and reneging on international obligations. We grew strong by improving our competitiveness. Our trade deficit is a major problem, but we can overcome it by making the right—not the wrong— policy moves. Trying to "save" jobs today in our *least* competitive industries by passing legislation that will assuredly cost us even more jobs in our most competitive industries is sheer folly.

America has traditionally been the world leader in promoting a free and open world trade system that has brought unprecedented prosperity, not only to our country, but to many others as well. Over the past 40 years, all administrations and the leaders of both parties in Congress have shared the conviction that expanding trade opportunities will bring higher living standards for all.

President Reagan is willing to take the lead with a forward-looking trade policy, but all those who have a stake in growing export markets have an obligation to help preserve the national consensus for expanding trade. Capitalism and democracy, which are inseparable, depend upon leadership from all citizens—not just leadership from government.

Look to the Future

The world has changed considerably in the last 40 years, but one thing that remains the same is that the rest of the globe looks to America's entrepreneurs, managers and workers to make the future happen just a little faster. No nation can take away our position of leadership—but we could give it away by succumbing to defeatism and fear.

President Reagan's trade policies are based on the belief that America's best days lie ahead—that our managers and workers can still go head-to-head with any in the world and come out on top. He rejects pessimism and I hope you do too. I invite you to join in a determined effort to expand international trading opportunities so that we can guarantee a better future not only for all Americans, but for all nations.

Clayton Yeutter is the United States trade representative.

"The mystical dream world of 'free trade' where the Reagan Administration stands enchanted is a world that never was and never will be."

viewpoint 108

Free Trade Would Not Solve the Trade Deficit

Lane Kirkland

The absence of a strong and predictable U.S. trade policy has contributed significantly to the sharp deterioration of the international economic position of the U.S. Scores of domestic industries and millions of American workers have been left defenseless against an onslaught of imports spurred by foreign governmental practices and the vagaries of macroeconomic policy. The consequences of this policy of neglect are being felt in all sectors of the economy through plant closings, bankruptcies, farm foreclosures, and recessionary unemployment levels. The Maine shoemaker, the Ohio machinist, the Kansas farmer, and even the high-tech worker in the Silicon Valley all have learned the lessons of international commerce—lessons learned not from textbooks or endless international negotiations, but from lost jobs, lost income, lost dignity, and devastated communities in every part of the nation.

In early 1986, as America was recording trade deficits that would have been unthinkable not too many years ago, Pres. Reagan, in his annual "Economic Report of the President" wrote: "Our international trade policy rests firmly on the foundation of free and open markets. The benefits of free trade are well known: it generates more jobs, a more productive use of a nation's resources, more rapid innovation, and high standards of living both for this nation and its trading partners." The Council of Economic Advisers, in the body of the report, elaborated on this theme, saying that job losses in the industrial sector were simply the result of improved efficiency and high wages, and that anyone who suggested otherwise has "an inadequate understanding of the benefits of trade."

For the millions of workers whose jobs were lost to imports or declining exports, this explanation

Lane Kirkland, "Reversing America's Decline in International Trade." Reprinted from USA TODAY MAGAZINE, March 1987. Copyright 1987 by the Society for the Advancement of Education.

provides little comfort. The shoeworker knows she is not overpaid at $6.00 an hour. The semiconductor worker knows he was efficient, but was still replaced by foreign production. With the Administration explanations, we have opened a sad new chapter in national policy of blame America first. The failures of government are papered over by blaming the victim.

Open Markets?

Where are the free and open markets on which Pres. Reagan bases his trade policy? Do they exist? Do they exist in Japan, the European Community, Brazil, Taiwan, or Mexico? Are free and open markets compatible with quotas, stringent inspection requirements, discriminatory standards, export subsidies and incentives, industrial targeting programs, buy-national policies, export performance requirements, barter agreements, and co-production requirements?

Where are the jobs this policy claims to generate? During 1986, unemployment stood at 7.2%, which translates into 8,400,000 Americans officially out of work and another 7,000,000 either too discouraged to seek employment or forced to work part-time. Of the nine post-World War II years with an unemployment rate above seven percent, five of those years were during the Reagan Administration.

The Department of Commerce estimated that in 1984 alone, 2,300,000 jobs in manufacturing were displaced by trade, with a net loss of 1,100,000 for the economy as a whole. In a study on displaced workers, the Bureau of Labor Statistics (BLS) reported that, between 1979 and 1984, 11,500,000 workers lost their jobs to plant closure, slack work, or layoffs. Twenty-five percent of those 11,500,000 are still looking for work, and 15% have left the labor force entirely.

The Administration believes that current trade policy generates a more productive use of this nation's resources and more rapid innovation. Is unemployment now productive? Does a highly skilled machinist contribute more to this nation's wealth in a retail store than he did making sophisticated machinery? How does innovation benefit the U.S. if new technology is licensed or sold to foreign concerns or the production of innovative goods is transferred overseas?

The Administration asserts that reliance on free-trade principles results in higher standards of living both for this nation and its trading partners. The average weekly earnings for U.S. production/non-supervisory employees declined more than nine percent from 1977 to 1985 in constant dollars. The reduction of employment in the manufacturing sector and the growth of jobs in the service sector have no doubt contributed to this decline. Average weekly earnings for manufacturing workers in 1985 reached $386. For workers in finance, insurance, and real estate, the average was $289. Workers in retail trade averaged $177, and employees in other types of service industries received $261. In the BLS study cited above, almost one-half of the displaced manufacturing workers who were fortunate enough to find alternative employment were forced to accept lower pay.

Few Benefits from Free Trade

Family share of national income also has undergone a shift. For the period 1980-84, the top 20% increased its share of national income by 1.3 percentage points while everyone else declined. Similarly, the benefits derived by other countries from U.S. reliance on free trade bear careful scrutiny. Who gains from the assembly of electronic components in less-developed countries?—not the worker frequently paid subsistence wages in an unhealthy or dangerous work environment, and prohibited from organizing and bargaining collectively. Even if one accepts the notion that free trade contributes to rising living standards, it is clear that any benefits are poorly distributed and that those who can least afford it bear the principal cost of this policy.

The mystical dream world of "free trade" where the Reagan Administration stands enchanted is a world that never was and never will be. I challenge anyone to name a single product, commodity, or service—including money—that moves in commerce under conditions which Adam Smith or David Ricardo would have recognized as free trade, unlevered by state policy or intervention. My confidence in that challenge is reinforced by the knowledge—to which Administration officials are selectively oblivious—that much of this world disavows a market economy altogether. Even more of it practices the most brutal form of protectionism—the protection of mercantile power and profit at the expense of the rights of working

people.

The growth of world trade did not reflect "open trading" so much as it represented directed trading in support of national development goals or the trade of multinational corporations which moved labor-intensive production to low-wage countries or which were drawn into direct foreign investment in order to sell in foreign markets.

A widely shared perspective among our trading partners has been, in effect, "buy from the U.S. what you need in order to acquire the technology and essentials to develop your own economy and treat the large U.S. market as a stepping stone to economies of scale and 'international competitiveness.'" However, "open," "closed," "free trade," and "protectionist" are all highly charged words that are not relevant in discussing international trade today. There is a good deal of trade, but it is, with the exception of the U.S., guided and regulated by national objectives.

The Deficit Grows

The dimensions of the problem are startling. The U.S. merchandise trade deficit in 1985 was three and one-half times higher than in 1980. For manufactured goods alone, America has gone from a surplus of $12,000,000,000 in 1980 to a deficit in 1985 that reached $113,000,000,000. During this period, exports fell 2.5% while imports of manufactured products shot up an astonishing 96%. In 1985, the import share of the U.S. market reached 50% for apparel, 23% for autos, 36% for machine tools, 25% for steel, and more than 75% for shoes. Deficits were experienced even in advanced products like semiconductors and telecommunications equipment.

"How does innovation benefit the U S if new technology is licensed or sold to foreign concerns?"

The numbers have become so large that there is a tendency to become numbed by the enormity of the shift in U.S. trade patterns and to find hope in any light that might appear on the trade horizon. For example, in reporting on the release of the February, 1986, trade numbers, the *Journal of Commerce's* front-page headline read: "U.S. Trade Deficit Shrinks." While lower than the deficits recorded in the previous few months, it still totaled $12,500,000,000, or $150,000,000,000 at an annual rate. Further, this "improving," deficit was 25% higher than what was recorded in February, 1985. The deficit for manufactured goods alone in February, 1986, was $10,000,000,000, or $120,000,000,000 on an annualized basis—higher than the record level reached in 1985.

Similarly, many are reassured that the U.S. trade problem soon will be history now that the dollar has begun to decline. What is frequently left unsaid is that the dollar remains some 40% higher against the currencies of our major trading partners than it was in 1980. In fact, the dollar has continued to appreciate somewhat against the currencies of Canada, Mexico, and Brazil. Even if the dollar stabilized or continued to fall—a scenario that is by no means certain—its impact on the U.S. trade deficit would not necessarily be large. Over the past five years, U.S. bilateral trade deficits grew substantially with countries like Taiwan and South Korea, who tie their currencies to the U.S.

Meanwhile, the American bilateral trade deficit with Japan more than doubled, even though the dollar had appreciated only marginally against the yen. Now that the dollar has fallen against the yen, there is similarly little assurance that this alone will reduce the U.S. deficit. In a 1986 article published in Japan's *Ashi Shimbun* newspaper, Japanese industry and government officials were quoted as saying that the change in the yen/dollar relationship probably would not affect Japanese exports significantly. As reasons, they cited Japan's export-oriented industrial structure and Japanese dominance in foreign markets which leave consumers little alternative. In addition, many U.S.-based multinational corporations which used to produce goods domestically now buy parts and half-finished products from Japan. On the import side, an official of the Ministry of Trade and Industry noted that primary products make up almost 70% of Japan's imports and stated, "nobody would want to eat more even if imported agricultural products become cheaper."

Changes in exchange rates will not by themselves provide the solution to America's trade crisis. Changes in trade law and policy urgently are needed to provide predictable relief to industries and workers injured by imports; to mandate governmental action when U.S. commerce is affected negatively by unreasonable or discriminatory practices of foreign governments; and to require countries that enjoy unwarranted trade surpluses with the U.S. and maintain barriers to American goods to begin to reduce those excessive surpluses.

Trade Reform

To ameliorate these problems, the AFL-CIO believes that any trade legislation should include trade law reform, providing more effective relief from injury by imports and protection from unfair trade practices; protection from unwarranted trade surpluses with the U.S; effective labor rights provisions; and adequate safeguards in any round of trade negotiations.

The "escape clause" (Section 301 of the Trade Act of 1974) was designed to provide a safety valve for those industries threatened with or experiencing serious injury from imports. Of the more than 55 cases filed since this provision became part of law, only 12 have resulted in any relief. Even in these cases, the relief never has been enough to allow the injured industry to recover fully from the import assault. To improve the functioning of this provision, the standard used by the International Trade Commission (ITC) in finding injury should be changed to the international standard, whereby imports must be a cause of serious injury or threat thereof. In the event of an affirmative finding of injury by the ITC, trade adjustment assistance should be provided automatically. We believe that, while the U.S. Trade Representative (USTR) should retain the discretion to modify that recommendation, including the negotiation of Orderly Marketing Agreements, the USTR must be required to take action to provide equivalent relief. In addition, petitioners should have the option of requesting the establishment of an industry advisory group made up of representatives from business, labor, and government to develop a plan to improve on industry's competitiveness. While the ITC should be required to take into account a group's plan in making its recommendation, the absence of a group or plan should not prejudice the ITC's decision.

Unfair Trade Practices

Section 301 provides the President with broad authority to take action against foreign countries whose practices burden, restrict, or discriminate against U.S. commerce. While we welcome decisions by the USTR to initiate actions against countries with unreasonable practices, the U.S. must go beyond what have been described as symbolic actions and vigorously pursue actions against practices that are harmful to U.S. domestic interests. . . .

"Changes in trade law and policy urgently are needed to provide predictable relief to industries and workers injured by imports."

Specific procedures should be adopted to provide certainty of response on the part of the U.S. government toward countries that maintain both excessive trade surpluses with the U.S and unreasonable or discriminatory trade practices. Countries so identified would be required to gradually reduce their surplus with the U.S. by opening their markets to American exports or reducing their own exports to this market. Failure to meet established goals would result in a series of escalating governmental responses.

Section 301 also should be amended to define failure on the part of a country to take steps to meet internationally recognized labor rights as contained in Title V of the Trade Agreements Act of 1984 as an unreasonable act, policy, or practice. Failure to take such steps would result in the denial of most-favored-nation treatment as long as that country remained out of compliance. We strongly believe that competitive advantage in trade should not be derived from the denial of the right to freedom of association, the refusal to ensure a safe work environment, the exploitation of child labor, or other such reprehensible practices.

Trade Negotiations

The AFL-CIO shares the reservations of many at home and abroad about the appropriateness of multilateral trade negotiations. Negotiations will not implement an effective national trade policy, correct the still overvalued dollar, or reduce America's huge trade deficit. Nevertheless, if negotiations are to take place, attention should be directed at the following areas:

• A major effort must be undertaken by national action and international negotiations to readjust currency values to more realistic levels and to bring some measure of stability to the exchange rate system. Such negotiations should be a precondition to any multilateral trade talks.

• The inadequacies of General Agreement on Tariffs and Trade (GATT) safeguard procedures need to be addressed. The U.S. should concentrate on exposing trade restrictive measures and should develop procedures for negotiating agreements that would bring some order and stability to trade in import-sensitive products, as well as products and commodities where worldwide excess capacity exists.

• Solutions to the serious problems faced by U.S. industry in the area of counterfeiting and intellectual property rights—such as computer programs, films, and recordings—should be a U.S. objective.

"The U.S. operates as if the trade-regulating measures of other countries do not exist or as if they were irrelevant."

• With regard to problems in services, solutions must be found through national action and sectoral negotiations. The emphasis on all-inclusive negotiations on trade in services is misplaced. The trade problems encountered by U.S. service industries are specific and quite diverse. Negotiations must be based on practical solutions for specific current problems so that the huge, diversified service industry will not be lumped together inappropriately in multilateral negotiations. U.S. law and practice establishing standards in the service sector must not be weakened.

• Instead of broad negotiations on investment rights, emphasis should be placed on encouraging domestic investment. As with trade in services, regulations concerning investment flows should not necessarily be viewed as barriers. The U.S. must not negotiate away domestic employment for business access to foreign markets.

A Realistic Framework

The U.S. needs to explore a more realistic general framework for coordinating world trade relationships in sectors characterized by global overcapacity and widespread import controls. The U.S. operates as if the trade-regulating measures of other countries do not exist or as if they were irrelevant in determining whether trade is likely to injure American workers and industries.

The temporary and often ineffective U.S. regulation of imports has not accomplished its purpose; other countries have dealt more effectively with international trade to promote industrial development and employment. At least when there is widespread import injury, and when trade problems have led the major importing countries to apply import restraint, the U.S. should negotiate an effective multilateral framework for allowing sectoral trade to take place in a rational manner, while preserving our vital industrial base and jobs.

Lane Kirkland is president of the American Federation of Labor-Congress of Industrial Organizations [AFL-CIO].

"We have at least as much right to protect American jobs as the Japanese and others have to protect theirs."

The US Should Restrict Japanese Imports

Lee A. Iacocca

Editor's note: The following viewpoint appears in two parts. Both parts are written by Lee A. Iacocca.

I

Japan and the United States have a very serious trade problem. Half of it is the fault of the Japanese, because they've been pillaging U.S. markets while shutting U.S. companies out of their market; they sell in the United States, but they will not buy there. The other half of the fault belongs to the United States, because it has its head in the sand. The federal budget deficit has gone out of sight and the dollar has gone so high that nobody can really afford U.S. goods anymore. Most important, the United States just doesn't have a trade policy at all.

Instead of a policy, the United States is trying to solve its trade problems by pressuring friends overseas to open up their economies like the United States did. It has been suggested that other countries cut taxes, discourage savings, spend more, lower their discount rates, and tear down all their trade barriers. There's one big problem with this, and it is called supply-side economics, better known in the trade as "Reaganomics." The United States is trying to tell other countries to run their economies like the United States has been running its own. Japan and Germany aren't that stupid; they're looking at the American experience. In just six years, the United States has more than doubled its national debt, and its trade deficits have totaled $623 billion in that time. It used to be the world's biggest creditor, and now it's the world's biggest debtor. The United States has lost about 2.8 million jobs to other countries. This is not a path others would want to follow.

A lot of demand in the United States has been created for foreign goods—but not American goods. This situation cuts back on jobs for U.S. workers. Foreign companies are having a field day in the American market right now. The United States was once the proud arsenal of democracy and champion of the industrial revolution, and it has now become one giant shopping mall. More and more, goods are *not* being produced in the United States—they are merely sold there. America has become the world's bazaar and everybody's welcome to come in, pitch a tent and peddle their wares. The rest of the world has become dependent on this market. . . .

The Auto Industry

An example of this dependency is the emerging auto industry right now in Korea. Most of the cars made there—in fact all of them—go directly from the factory to the docks. They have to; when people are paid $2 an hour to build cars, it's a little difficult to get them to buy those cars. Therefore, most of Korea's auto output is exported to North America. The Koreans learned that game from the Japanese, and they learned it well. Toyota is the only company that makes money in the Japanese home market. The Japanese car companies barely break even in the rest of the world, except for one country: the United States. For years, virtually 100 percent of the profits for the Japanese auto industry as a whole have come from one market—the United States. Now, with currency changes such as the appreciation of the yen, those profits are going to be smaller. An interesting thing is happening: with the currency moving in "favor of the United States" by more than 67 percent, the Japanese have raised car prices by 15 percent only. That indicates two things: how much profit they've been making in this market and taking home and how badly they need to hang on to that share of the U.S. market to keep their factories running and their people employed.

The car industry used to be the "Big Three." Now it's becoming the "Big Thirty." Everybody's in the U.S. market because that is where the profits are. It doesn't matter whether one is Japanese or Korean or Yugoslavian or Lower Slobovian, for that matter. One must sell cars in the United States if one expects to make any real money.

The United States is not simply a good market for cars, but for a wide range of products: stereos, cameras, television sets, computers—just about *any* product. Thirty-nine percent of Japan's total exports come to the United States. Korea sends 36 percent of its total exports to the United States, Canada sends 81 percent, and Mexico 87 percent. The Third World as a whole sends nearly one third of all its exports to the United States. That's not bad, but it's a one-way street. The United States has big deficits in goods with seventeen out of the top twenty trading partners dealing with the United States.

These deficits are actually IOUs, and they are to be paid back some day, somehow. Annually, the current deficit with the rest of the world roughly equals a total of all personal savings in the United States for a full year. If one were a banker, it could be said that this is a 100 percent lien on all the savings of the United States, or better yet, it's actually a lien on the futures of the children.

The deck has been stacked against the United States. There hasn't been fair trade, or any policies coming out of Washington to offer fair trade, and some don't seem to understand what "fair" means. The Japanese never use that word; they use another word—"harmony"—in trade. That means: "let's get along" or "let's not change anything." Some things are going to have to change when the Japanese have a $60 billion annual surplus with the United States, $26 billion annually in cars alone, and then keep out U.S. imports. They keep out citrus, they keep out beef; they say they need to protect their farmers. They have quotas on almost everything: cat food, wine, walnuts, chocolate, and baseball bats, anything with value added.

Value added means jobs and labor that make a product. For example, potatoes are permissible as imports for Japan, but not potato chips, because it takes labor to slice them; tomatoes are okay but not tomato puree, because somebody has to squeeze the tomatoes. Hides are okay but not leather, because somebody's got to tan the hides, and logs are okay but not plywood, because somebody's got to cut it.

Japan's Colony?

The United States ships Japan raw materials; Japan ships the United States finished goods. That is the classic definition of a colony. The United States will become a colony again if it gives up its industrial base and merely relies on services to save the economy. Only a couple of years ago, it was thought that services and high technology would save the

United States, but now high technology may not be the way out. What's so scary is that it's not just one or two isolated industries in trouble.

Look who's been going to Washington, D.C. lately to ask for help. In 1979 it was steel; in 1980 it was the auto industry, especially Chrysler. Machine tools went in 1981; telecommunications went in 1982. Next, even computers showed up, then textiles, then the oil companies. Now, even the farmers, the most productive farmers in the world, are going broke. It's hard to believe.

Soon there won't be anybody left to service. If the industrial sector goes down the tubes, who's going to buy the hamburgers? Whose laundry can be taken in? Somebody had better start thinking about that, because it's basic.

"The United States needs a trade policy that's first and foremost fair to America and Americans."

The largest bank in the world is no longer City Corporation of America; it's Dai Ichi Kangyo of Japan. In fact, four of the five largest banks in the world are now in Japan, and thirteen of the largest twenty-five banks in the world are now Japanese. Just six years ago, there was only one Japanese bank in the top ten.

How did those Japanese banks get so rich so quickly? They rolled up on the wave of Japanese industry and Japanese exports. Also, they kept their currency undervalued for many years, and got a big jump in its value in the past year; that turned right into wealth.

The way to ruin the United States is to give up on basic industries. It's necessary to break the notion that this country can get along without factories, mills, and oil wells.

Six years ago Chrysler was literally dying and some people—a lot of people—said, "Hey, that's the system, boys. It's your own fault. You're lousy managers and you must pay the price." But Chrysler didn't make gas double in price overnight and it didn't make interest rates double along with gas overnight. The two factors that fuel the automobile business are the price of gas and the price of money. They both went up 100 percent. Yet people at Chrysler were told they were lousy managers. No manager in any business can manage swings like that. A 10 or 15 percent change up or down can be handled, but nobody can handle a 100 percent swing.

American businesses need to stick together and convince Congress to write a trade policy allowing U.S. business to compete again. The policy could start with self-interest. Congress should simply ask itself, "What's in our self-interest in this deal?" A deficit with Japan approaching $60 billion is simply not in America's self-interest, while the $60 billion for which the Japanese depend on the American market is not in Japan's self-interest, either. It's not good business planning to have so many eggs in one basket, because the basket will get so heavy that it will drop and they won't like the mess on the floor. Therefore it's in the interest of both countries to narrow the trade gap—now.

There needs to be a strategic goal to reduce the trade deficit soon, maybe 10 percent a year, then 15, then 18, and then 20. The politicians are yelling, "You can't lay down rules because the other guy will retaliate." The United States is in the red and is being duped—yet it's afraid of retaliation? Don't be afraid of retaliation; other countries need the U.S. market too much.

The United States has become the leader of the free world by default. The others have depended on it and its market too much since World War II. The United States is still the leader, even though its leadership is dwindling. Somewhere along the line the leader has to set some rules and give some direction. It used to be said that the world would become economically interdependent, and that sounded good because it was supposed to bring countries closer together. Trade would wipe out war, because everybody's self-interest would be linked together. However, that's not what is happening. Instead, a lot of countries are rushing blindly backward toward the kind of mindless mercantilism that once tore this world apart.

"America's trade door has been wide open and Japan's has been barely cracked enough to get your foot in."

The United States doesn't seem to have any trade policy at all. But overseas, governments and businesses are tied together too tightly. They work hand in hand to grab as much loot as they can to return to the mother country, just as in the colonial days. That's not the kind of trade policy that is good for America. Leadership is needed from the U.S. government to make things a little fairer. The United States needs to compete fairly with people overseas, but not equally. One area in which the United States can't compete and shouldn't even want to compete is how much the wage rate can be lowered.

Chrysler is asking some of its workers to agree to more practical labor agreements so that it can compete with foreign companies, and the unions are doing it. They don't like it, but they're doing it, because they want to compete. Mostly, they want to save their jobs. However, it would not be fair to ask

Chrysler employees to throw away their standard of living and give up their hopes for their children because somebody halfway around the world is happy to get $1 an hour.

The United States needs a trade policy that's first and foremost fair to America and Americans and fair to U.S. trading partners. That gives other countries a fair share of the U.S. market if the United States receives a fair share of theirs. Moreover, the United States needs a trade policy that maintains a strong American industrial base as much as it needs a strong defense establishment. The country can't survive without either of those.

II

Nothing makes me see red quicker than the defeatist attitude of some free-trade purists who say that changing America's doormat trade policies would cost more jobs than it would save.

For years we've heard it: "No matter what other countries do to shut out our products or dump their goods in this country, we can't do anything to protect ourselves or the other guys will retaliate and we'll lose even more jobs."

And whenever I hear another verse to that old tune I wonder whether we've finally lost our guts in this country. It sounds like a boxer who has just lost 14 straight rounds, and goes into the 15th saying, "Gee, I hope I don't make him mad!"

It's time we put these Chicken Littles on the spot and made them prove that the cure is worse than the disease. And I want some real-world proof, not just a recital of the same old textbook theories we all memorized in school. Where are the American jobs that have been created or saved by our cumulative $623 billion trade deficit over the past six years? Give me a number.

We know about the jobs lost, we can count them: the current level of imports is costing us conservatively 460,000 auto jobs, 370,000 apparel jobs, 280,000 in high-tech components, 130,000 in consumer electronics, 67,000 in machine tools, and 66,000 in steel. And these numbers don't include the ripple effect through the economy.

Costly Imports

The government's own rule of thumb is that for every billion-dollar increase in our trade deficit, 25,000 American jobs are lost. This year, our trade deficit could be as much as $50 billion worse than last year. That's a million and a quarter more jobs lost in just 12 months, directly attributable to the trade deficit.

Show me the number of jobs that this $50 billion has created or protected.

Sure, we're creating more jobs in the United States, but they're mostly service jobs which usually pay much less than the industrial jobs we've been losing.

The real issue is how many jobs would we have today if we hadn't let the trade deficit get out of control; and, by that measure, job creation in this decade has not been a roaring success.

One other thing they never bring up when they talk about trade and jobs in Japan. America's trade door has been wide open and Japan's has been barely cracked enough to get your foot in. Yet Japan has a steady unemployment rate of under 3 percent while ours is stuck at around 7 percent.

So much for the notion that tight trade rules cost jobs.

An Important Market

But still, the purists say the other guys can play that game, but we can't. We'd start a trade war and everyone—especially the United States—would lose.

That's baloney! The other guys need the American market more than we need their goods. The American market drives the whole world's economy. If you expect to make any profit in world trade today you have to sell in America. There's no place else to go because everybody else has drawn a line on imports to keep their people in jobs.

Look at the record. About 30 percent of the total exports of the whole Third World come to America. We take 39 percent of Japan's exports, 36 percent of Korea's, 81 percent of Canada's, and 87 percent of Mexico's, to name just a few.

"It's time to quiet down all the nervous Nellies who keep telling us that getting tough on trade will cost us jobs."

How important is the American market? Japan's [1985] trade surplus with the United States accounted for virtually 100 percent of its total worldwide trade surplus of $50 billion. They may be the greatest traders in the world right now, but they only break even with the rest of the world. Their total worldwide trade surplus comes from just one market—America.

Now, with that kind of dependence on just one market, the Japanese and the others aren't stupid. They aren't going to bite the hand that feeds them. They aren't going to retaliate if we insist on some sensible·and fair trade policies that help us keep a few jobs in the United States.

Dependent on the US

The whole world is overly dependent on the American market, and that's not good for anybody. But we at least ought to use that dependence to our own advantage. We ought to use it to force the other guys to play fair with us because we have at least as much right to protect American jobs as the Japanese

and others have to protect theirs.

For a long time now, the workers in infant industries in emerging countries have had special protection under international trade agreements so they could have time to get competitive with the workers in the older industrial nations. We've been buying all they can ship to America without insisting that they open their markets to us, and in the process we've sacrificed a lot of American jobs.

Our trading partners don't need that kind of special protection any more. In fact, the brand-new factory in Korea has an enormous advantage over an established plant in America. Because technology today is so easily available and it changes so rapidly, a new factory—no matter where it is—will always be more productive. And when you add in lower wage rates, and government policies that promote exports, and a gang of trade barriers that keep our products out of their markets, there's no reason to feel sorry for workers in Asia anymore. It's our people who need help.

Stable Employment

We don't operate on the day-labor mentality in this country anymore. A job is a long-term commitment involving the worker, the company, and even the government. Stable employment is the most important part of economic growth. Japan knows that, and that's why Japanese trade policies have just one major objective: hang onto the jobs. Keep the unemployment rate so low that it's even tough to measure.

But the people making our trade policies and fiscal policies seem to believe that jobs take care of themselves.

The supply-siders didn't notice our wide-open trade door, for example, when they put their trickle-down policies in place. Our fiscal policies may have put more money in the pockets of American consumers, but foreign trade practices and the high American dollar gave foreign companies a much better shot at that extra money.

So the supply-side theory has been turned upside down. We've really had "demand-side" economics. We've created lots of American demand for foreign goods, but we've forgotten about American supply, and that's where the American jobs are.

It's been a good deal for the consumers (at least the ones who are working). It's been a great deal for our trading partners. It's helped control inflation. But at what cost? At the cost of millions of American jobs!

So it's time to quiet down all the nervous Nellies who keep telling us that getting tough on trade will cost us jobs. It won't. But the fear to act will guarantee that we'll just keep shipping more and more Americans jobs offshore.

Lee A. Iacocca is chairman of the board for the Chrysler Corporation.

"The debate on U.S. competitiveness needs to shift its focus from Japan-bashing to the root causes of America's economic difficulties."

viewpoint 110

The US Should Not Restrict Japanese Imports

Yoshi Tsurumi

By now it should be clear that a lower dollar is no panacea for America's trade imbalance. Two years after it peaked in early 1985, the dollar has declined more than 40 percent against the Japanese yen, the German mark, and other major currencies. Yet the dollar's plunge has done little to reduce the trade deficit, which last year reached a record $148 billion.

No single country has taken as much blame for this widening imbalance as Japan, which last year registered a $56-billion trade surplus with the United States. Japan's share of the U.S. trade deficit has remained more or less constant since the 1970s, at around 30 percent. But, lately, resentment over this large surplus, which critics attribute partly to unfair trade practices, has been mounting. "The level of frustration with Japan is higher than I have ever seen," Clayton Yeutter, the United States trade representative, said in March [1987]. This frustration is evident in calls for more "voluntary" restrictions on the export of Japanese goods, White House efforts to block the sale of an electronics subsidiary—foreign-owned—to one of Japan's electronics giants, and a bill before Congress that would require the president to retaliate against countries whose large trade surpluses are determined to be the result of practices that close markets to U.S. products. Japan is also under pressure to open more of its markets to U.S. goods and to help buy the United States out of its trade slump through increased consumption of those goods.

The tendency to blame Japan first may be politically convenient but it does not go to the heart of the matter and, more important, it is likely to exacerbate the problem. In April 1987 the Reagan administration finally joined the congressional

chorus for bashing Japan and slapped punitive import tariffs on an assortment of electronic goods. In turn, Japan is poised to take retaliatory measures. No one doubts that the playing field of U.S.-Japanese trade relations is not entirely level, but which way does it slope? For if Japan restricts its imports of U.S. agricultural products, the United States protects its steel, automobile, textile, and microchip industries against Japanese competition. According to the Institute of International Economics, about $5 billion worth of Japanese exports are being restrained by various U.S. quotas and regulations. Were Japan to drop all barriers to trade, this same study concludes, its trade surplus with the United States would only be trimmed by about the same amount. In other words, if all were perfectly fair, little difference would it make.

Counterproductive Pressure

U.S. pressures on Japan are already proving to be counterproductive. The rising yen has left Japan vulnerable to other export-oriented Asian economies whose currencies have not appreciated against the dollar. As its volume of exports declines, Japan is even resorting to plant closings, layoffs, and relocation overseas—measures it has traditionally avoided. Unemployment rose to 3 percent in January—the highest level since 1953. Such conditions only aggravate social tensions and strengthen the hand of "localists" against any further accommodations. To cope with this economic slowdown, Japan, naturally enough, is not increasing its consumption of American-made goods but rather is buying fewer imports generally.

The clues to America's worsening trade deficit with Japan lie closer to home. The United States has long believed that economic success does not require any special effort, a belief perhaps understandable for a nation that was catapulted into a position of economic hegemony at the end of World War II.

Yoshi Tsurumi, "The U.S. Trade Deficit with Japan," *World Policy Journal*, Vol. IV #2, Spring 1987. Reprinted with permission.

This belief is now gradually giving way to an increasing recognition of the need to enhance U.S. competitiveness, evident in calls for more research and development, expanded investment, and worker retraining. Yet, as we shall see, even these proposals skirt the central issue: the need for the federal and state governments to assume a more active role in managing economic development. In this and other respects, learning from the Japanese is likely to prove more useful than blaming them. . . .

"A closer look at the U.S. trade deficit with Japan . . . reveals it has less to do with foul play and more to do with such things as comparative advantage and differences in product quality."

A closer examination of the U.S. trade deficit with Japan reveals a picture quite different from the one that is commonly perceived. To casual observers, Japan appears to buy little from the United States and to sell it much. In reality, Japan buys quite a lot from the United States. After Canada, Japan is the second largest importer of U.S. goods, purchasing about 14 percent of America's total exports. Japan imports more U.S. goods than Mexico, the United Kingdom, and West Germany combined. Thirty-three percent of all U.S. agricultural exports are purchased by Japan—three times more than the Soviet Union buys—including 70 percent of America's beef exports, 40 percent of its citrus fruit exports, and 18 percent of its tobacco exports. Moreover, although Japan's share of America's $148-billion trade deficit amounted to $56 billion last year, this was partly offset from U.S. net surpluses of about $10-$15 billion in the service-trade sector with Japan: receipts from technical royalties, investment income, transportation fees, and tourism. (Over 7 million Japanese tourists visited the United States in 1986 alone.)

Trade Deficit Factors

A closer look at the U.S. trade deficit with Japan also reveals that it has less to do with foul play and more to do with such things as comparative advantage and differences in product quality, consumer preference, levels of consumer spending, and the relative importance the two countries place on defense spending. On the basis of technological complexity, U.S. and Japanese products fall into three categories: low-tech goods, including agricultural products and other primary commodities such as coal, forestry products, scrap iron, and processed foods; medium-tech products, including consumer and industrial goods like automobiles,

steel, machine-tools, textiles, photocopiers, and cameras; and high-tech products, including pharmaceuticals, computers, industrial robots, precision medical equipment, biotech-related products, telecommunication equipment, microchips, and aircraft.

In terms of price and quality, the United States commands absolute advantage over Japan in most low-tech products; it generates a $16-billion annual trade surplus with Japan in this group. Japan generally commands absolute advantage over the United States in many medium-tech products, enjoying a $70-$80 billion surplus in this area. The United States and Japan split their relative advantage among high-tech products. The United States exports many passenger aircraft to Japan, and American-made satellites and accompanying high-speed communication gears are still largely superior to Japanese brands. Cray Corporation, an American firm, outsells Fujitsu and Hitachi supercomputers, even in Japan. However, Japan enjoys comparative advantages in microchips and in the field of civilian telecommunications equipment, such as telephones and electronic switchboards. In fact, it was largely on the basis of Japan's dominance of the U.S. microchip market that it generated a $6-$7 billion trade surplus in high-tech products last year [1986].

Japanese and American Consumers

In the utopian world of free trade and comparative advantages, the United States would export mostly low- and some high-tech products to Japan, and Japan would export mostly medium-tech products to the United States. If mutual demand for these products were the same, if there were no market restraints, and if American-made low- and high-tech products were internationally competitive in price, quality, delivery, and other customer services, there would be no U.S. trade deficit with Japan. But these conditions, of course, do not prevail. First of all, Japanese consumers traditionally have been low spenders, saving more than twice as much of their personal disposable income as their American counterparts. Moreover, the United States has a population twice as large as Japan's, which means its absolute demand for goods is greater. It also means that, on a per-capita basis, both countries actually import about the same amount from each other.

As for market restraints, both the United States and Japan restrict imports of many low- and high-tech products. In the area of high-tech products, where the two countries enjoy rough trade parity, the United States often restricts imports because many of these products are closely related to defense procurements. On the other hand, Japan is suspected of erecting barriers to the importation of U.S. supercomputers: despite its acknowledged technological lead over Japan in this area, the United States has only 23 percent of the Japanese market.

Since both liberals and conservatives in the United States are anxious about the future of U.S. Japanese high-tech competition, they are pressuring Congress and the White House to further limit Japanese access to the American market and, at the same time, to pry open the Japanese market.

Most of Japan's trade barriers affect imports of low-tech products. Twenty-two out of the 23 product categories restricted for import to Japan are mainly agricultural products. In Japan, farmers wield a disproportionate amount of influence, given that they constitute only about 10 percent of the total population. They benefit from the fact that the power of elected national officials in Japan derives from the Lower Diet, whose seat allocation has changed very little since 1947 when much of the country's population was living out the war in rural regions. Japan's farmer-bureaucrat alliance is not only powerful but quite prepared to jeopardize the country's overall relations with the United States in pursuit of its interests. . . .

"America's trade problems . . . cannot be solved by quarreling over trade barriers because these problems are largely made in America."

Japan is blamed for "unfair" and "unlevel" competition but, as a former assistant U.S. trade representative commented, "Japan is the metaphor for the loss of our competitive edge." Japan, it is true, needs to eliminate its obsolete and cumbersome requirements for product specifications, product tests, and customs clearance procedures that handicap many medium- and high-tech imports; eventually it will have to open all its markets, especially in the agricultural sector. For these restrictions inevitably and unnecessarily politicize U.S.-Japanese economic relations. But even by the most optimistic reckoning, the removal of all Japanese tariff and nontariff barriers might increase U.S. annual exports to Japan by $10-$15 billion. This would still leave a bilateral trade deficit of $40-$45 billion. Moreover, this assumes, among other things, that the United States would be the only beneficiary of a more open Japanese market. But, for instance, if all barriers to primary commodities were removed, the United States would still face severe competition from Canada, Thailand, and Argentina, among others.

As for medium-tech products, which account for most of the trade deficit with Japan, the only real barriers to U.S. imports are quality and consumer satisfaction, and these obviously cannot be negotiated away. Moreover, any gains by the removal of Japanese barriers in this area would be offset by increases in Japanese exports to the United States with the removal of voluntary export restraints. Finally, in the area of high-tech products, one of the greatest barriers to increased U.S. sales is Pentagon distortions of the commercial market and restrictions on the sale of sensitive technology. America's trade problems, in other words, cannot be solved by quarreling over trade barriers because these problems are largely made in America, born of twin failures: a defense-first style of planning and obsolete management practices. . . .

Intertwined Trading Systems

Given today's multilateral, interdependent trading systems, it makes little economic sense to single out bilateral trade deficits such as the one between the United States and Japan. The trans-Pacific trading structure is already so intertwined among nations that a unilateral reduction in U.S. imports of Japanese goods could, for instance, wipe out the U.S. trade surplus with Australia. With fewer goods to export to the United States, Japan might reduce its imports of industrial raw materials from Australia. Australia, in turn, would have less to spend on goods from the United States because of reduced income from exports to Japan. All would suffer. Similarly, if Japan were to retaliate for U.S. actions by shifting its purchases of grain from the United States to Thailand, Australia, or Canada, the overall U.S. trade deficit would grow and the U.S. agricultural sector would plunge deeper into recession.

The Reagan administration is placing an increasing emphasis on talking down the dollar, not just as a way of making U.S. goods more competitive but also in the hope of forcing Japan to reflate its economy. This is proving to be counterproductive. U.S. pressure for a weaker dollar and a stronger yen plays into the very hands of those in Japan who resist any further accommodation with the United States. Rapid yen appreciation has damaged the export competitiveness of many firms and regions that make standard crafts and manufactures. Here Korea, Taiwan, Singapore, and other Asian nations whose currencies have not appreciated against the dollar now enjoy a competitive advantage. This situation has not only depressed the Japanese economy—GNP grew by only 2.5 percent in 1986, well below the 4.7 percent of the previous year—but is creating a rift between "localists" and "internationalists." Small to medium-sized manufacturers, local merchants, and employees whose export-related interests are crushed by the rising yen are joining the coalition of farmers and bureaucrats who stand to lose most by opening Japan's markets and dismantling its consumer and industrial regulations.

If the United States continues to talk down the dollar against the yen, the bureaucrat-farmer-localist alliance that holds enormous political power in Japan could very well seek retaliation against the United States, perhaps through the financial leverage Japan now wields with its massive investments in that country. If Japan were to abruptly curtail its capital outflows to the United States, this would put upward pressure on U.S. interest rates and possibly plunge the U.S. economy into a recession. For that reason, the United States needs to be more mindful of the imperiled internationalists, who are increasingly represented in the ruling Liberal Democratic party (LDP). Even though the LDP won an overwhelming victory in elections held last July, candidates in rural areas encountered heightened opposition. Liberal Democrats, as a result, are turning increasingly for support to internationalist-oriented urban voters. But continued demands on the part of the United States for export restraints and a strong yen could work against this budding realignment that, in the end, offers the best chance for improved U.S.-Japanese relations.

This is not to say that an adjustment of the dollar-yen relationship is unnecessary or unwelcome, only that it must be more carefully managed. A dollar-yen exchange rate stabilized around the 165 yen level would benefit both the United States and Japan. It would allow Tokyo to put into effect stimulative domestic measures to offset any deflationary effects of reduced export activity. And without the uncertainty that now hangs over the yen, Japanese industries would be able to plan for a more orderly expansion of their overseas manufacturing and service activities, including those in the United States.

"The United States needs to recognize that it can no longer dictate the rules of international competition."

Such expanded Japanese operations in the United States would mean greater U.S. job creation and more competitive American-made products. As it is, Japanese firms lead all other foreign firms in the United States in their export of U.S.-made products, accounting for 12 percent of total exports. Unfortunately, the American business and political leadership treats this expansion of Japanese business activity in the United States somewhat as an enemy invasion. Consider, for example, Congress and the Pentagon's reaction to Fujitsu's offer to purchase the ailing Fairchild Semiconductor Corporation, a subsidiary of Schlumberger Ltd. When Schlumberger, a French firm, acquired Fairchild in 1979, there was no outcry in the United States. But Fujitsu's recent offer triggered sudden concerns that the sale would jeopardize U.S. security interests,

since Fairchild supplies the military with computer chips. Bowing to pressure, Fujitsu announced it would not proceed with the purchase. Ironically, this decision may now make U.S. national security even more dependent on the import of microchips, whereas Fujitsu's purchase of Fairchild might have helped bolster the company's sagging technological capabilities.

Increased Japanese business activity in the United States would also be likely to increase the sale of U.S.-made goods and services to Japanese firms operating here and to their subsidiaries abroad. This could help restore balance to multilateral trading in the Pacific Basin and throughout the world. Meanwhile, continued outflows of capital and technology from Japan to the United States would foster stronger ties between American and Japanese firms in the Pacific and elsewhere. A stable dollar-yen rate would also benefit Pacific nations who rely on Japanese purchases of their goods to service their debts. For such countries as Korea and the Philippines, which have yen-based debts, a lower yen is especially crucial if they are to avoid the austerity measures and consequent economic contraction that the high dollar has meant for Latin America—contraction that has closed one market after another to U.S. exports.

The Challenge To Be Competitive

The debate on U.S. competitiveness needs to shift its focus from Japan-bashing to the root causes of America's economic difficulties. The Japanese challenge should be met with the same seriousness that Sputnik was 30 years ago, when the Soviet satellite launching shocked the United States out of complacency. Congress and the federal government subsequently cut loose from laissez-faire dogma and initiated a nationwide effort to improve the quality of science education, to accelerate space and scientific research, and to work jointly with business and universities to put a man on the moon before the Soviet Union did. By contrast, few Americans today even recognize the seriousness of the "microchip shock" and its homegrown causes.

The United States must understand that it cannot regain its competitiveness without adopting new ways of doing business. There is nothing wrong with pressing Japan to open markets that remain closed, but the United States cannot expect simply to bully its way to competitiveness. The United States needs to recognize that it can no longer dictate the rules of international competition, especially now that it is so dependent on Japanese capital to revive its industries. In fact, by virtue of its economic efficiency and manufacturing dominance, Japanese-style strategic planning and corporate management practices are being adopted by Asia's newly industrializing countries. Rather than fight these rules, the United States would be wise to adapt them to its own particular needs.

At a minimum, a stronger government role is required to encourage more flexible and competitive behavior on the part of labor and management, to set national goals and priorities for the allocation of scarce resources, to ensure that the different components of a competitive strategy—from worker retraining to research and development—are properly funded and well coordinated with each other, and to assist those parts of the country that lag behind other parts. These are all aspects of what can be called strategic planning. . . .

Learn from the Japanese

Ultimately, of course, only corporations can learn to manage themselves better. Rather than knocking Japanese companies' success, U.S. firms would do better to learn from the Japanese example. This is not as alien as some would believe. American firms are already demonstrating that it is not essential to be Japanese to become competitively lean and productive. IBM, Johnson & Johnson, Procter & Gamble, Black & Decker, Lincoln Industries, and Xerox have all responded effectively to the challenge of foreign competition by making fundamental changes in corporate behavior. Black & Decker, for instance, galvanized its managers and employees to work together bringing out new products more quickly and at more competitive prices. And Xerox's copier division underwent the corporate equivalent of a cultural revolution, cutting its component rejection rate from a whopping 8,000 parts per million in the early 1980s to 1,300 parts per million by 1985.

Getting America's own house in order, of course, will not solve all the problems of U.S.-Japanese trade. But it will allow whatever trade complaints there are to be addressed on their merits. It will also facilitate the type of U.S.-Japanese cooperative management that the growing trans-Pacific economy now requires.

Yoshi Tsurumi is president of the Pacific Basin Center Foundation and professor of international business at Baruch College, City University of New York.

"Comparable worth [is] the best way of producing economic justice for women workers who are shunted into the lowest-paid jobs."

viewpoint **111**

Comparable Worth Promotes Equality

Sylvia Ann Hewlett

Say the words *modern working women,* and our minds immediately conjure up images of superwomen, those female anchorpersons and executive vice-presidents so beloved by the media. Barbara Walters, Mary Cunningham, and Sherry Lansing are our modern heroines, and the press would have us believe that the underbrush is full of glamorous career women with six-figure incomes.

Women in the Work Force

Fortune magazine runs a spread on vivacious Linda Taylor. A graduate of Harvard's Business School, Linda is in her mid-thirties and on the fast track. She has just been promoted to chief investment officer of the United Mine Workers' $2.3 billion pension and health fund and now earns more than $100,000 a year. Linda is also the mother of three children. To keep her household running smoothly, Linda employs a staff of three—housekeeper, nanny, and weekend substitute (who takes over housekeeping and child care on Saturday and Sunday). The annual payroll of Linda's domestic staff totals $27,000.

Forbes has a story on dynamic Lorraine Mecca. Five years ago this enterprising thirty-four-year-old former English teacher invested $25,000 from her divorce settlement in her fledgling Micro D Inc. of Fountain Valley, California—a wholesale operation that sells computer software. In the first nine months of 1983 Micro D had sales of $50 million and a net of $859,000. The company went public in July 1984, raising $25 million. Lorraine is now a wealthy woman.

Would that Linda and Lorraine were representative of working women in our society. Unfortunately reality is a lot less glamorous. Despite the enormous expansion of the female labor force in recent

years—the number of women working has doubled since 1960—there has been little improvement in women's economic position.

Only 7 percent of employed women in America work in managerial positions, and only 10 percent earn more than $20,000 a year. Three-quarters of American working women continue to be employed in traditional "women's jobs" and spend their time waiting on tables, typing letters, cutting hair, emptying bedpans, and cleaning offices. Most are badly paid. In 1984, 1 out of every 4 women earned less than $10,000 a year when working full time. In many cases, some women's salaries fail to lift them above the poverty line, and this produces much hardship in a day and age when women's wages no longer constitute pin money. Today 45 percent of working women are single, divorced, separated, or widowed and have no option but to take prime economic responsibility for themselves (and often their children). The low earning power of women helps explain why 35 percent of single mothers fall below the poverty line.

A critical measure of how well women are doing in the labor market is the wage gap, which is the difference between male and female earnings. The wage gap in America is extremely wide and has not shifted in fifty years.

In 1939, when Franklin D. Roosevelt was president, *Gone with the Wind* was awarded the Academy Award as best picture, and Joe DiMaggio won the batting title, women earned sixty-three cents to a man's dollar. Presidents have come and gone, *Gone with the Wind* is on cable TV, and DiMaggio is a legend. But women's earning power hasn't changed much. Today women earn sixty-four cents to a man's dollar (August 1985 figure released by the Bureau of the Census). We have women astronauts and women vice-presidential candidates—indeed, fully 45 percent of the U.S. labor force is now female—but despite all these changes, the gap between male and female earnings is as wide as it was half a century ago.

In 1984 the median earnings of women who worked full time year-round was $14,479, while similarly employed men earned $23,218. A woman with four years of college still earns less than a male high school dropout. . . .

The American Wage Gap

One deeply disturbing fact is that the wage gap in America is wider—and more stubborn—than in other advanced industrial countries. As British economist Peter Sloane describes it, "in most countries for which data are available the average gender wage differential narrowed significantly during the 1970s"; only in the United States did the sex wage differential "remain fixed as if through some divine law." For example, in Sweden, where women are among the highest-paid in Europe, women earned just over 81 percent of male earnings in 1980, up from 71 percent in 1970. And in Britain, where women are among the lowest-paid in Europe, women's wages as a percentage of men's increased from 54 percent in 1970 to 66 percent in 1982. This narrowing of the gap between male and female earning power can be seen in most advanced democracies. In Italy women's wages as a percentage of men's wages increased from 74 percent in 1968 to 86 percent in 1982; in West Germany women's wages rose from 69 percent in 1968 to 73 percent in 1982; in France they rose from 76 percent in 1964 to 78 percent in 1982; and in Denmark they rose from 74 percent in 1968 to 86 percent in 1982. Traditional Catholic societies as well as Scandinavian welfare states have made more progress than we have on this critical front.

"The wage gap in America is wider— and more stubborn—than in other advanced industrial countries."

The low earning power of American women workers is particularly surprising when one takes into consideration the educational picture. American women are the best-educated in the world. Of current four-year college students 52 percent are female, and half of all master's degrees and a quarter of all professional degrees go to women. Indeed, the average woman worker is now slightly better educated than the average male worker, having completed a median of 12.65 years of schooling, compared to 12.57 for men. In other countries women continue to lag behind men in educational attainment. In Britain women make up only 39 percent of students in higher education, in Italy the figure is 41 percent, and in France it is 45 percent. One would therefore expect the wage gap in

these countries to be wider, not narrower. All of which adds to the mystery of why American women do so badly in the workplace.

Perhaps the biggest surprise is that elite women are not closing the economic gender gap. Census data show that more women hold executive and professional positions than ever before—the percentage of managerial jobs held by women rose from 14.5 percent in 1960 to 28.9 percent in 1980—yet over these two decades, when executive women made such impressive numerical gains, the wage gap between men and women executives actually widened. In 1960 women managers earned 58 percent of the male wage; in 1980 they earned 55 percent. Women are simply not making it into upper management; they remain heavily concentrated in the lower half of the corporate pyramid. According to Barbara Everitt Bryant, a senior vice-president at the Market Opinion Research Company in Detroit, women make up about 50 percent of entry management and 25 percent of middle management. But although business began recruiting and promoting women in substantial numbers in the early 1970s—far enough back to give them time for considerable career advancement—they account for only a tiny percentage of upper management. Estimates are in the 1 to 2 percent range. There seems to be a revolving door for women at the bottom of the managerial career ladder.

A final piece of depressing news is that the difference between starting salaries for men and women has widened in recent years. Gordon Green, a demographer at the Bureau of the Census, has found that the wages of white women entering the job market were 3 percentage points farther behind comparable white men in 1980 than they were in 1970. This is "despite the growth of affirmative action and educational gains by women." . . .

Sex Segregation

Despite the changes of recent years, the United States labor market is still largely segregated by sex. In 1982, 50 percent of employed women worked in only 20 occupations—out of the 427 occupations detailed by the United States Department of Labor. More than half of all employed women worked in occupations which were 75 percent female, and 22 percent of employed women were in jobs that were more than 95 percent female. Women still account for 99 percent of secretaries, 97 percent of typists, and 96 percent of all registered nurses.

Contrary to popular opinion, the entry of women into professional and blue-collar jobs has *not* reduced the overall degree of segregation. This is because the movement of a few women into predominantly male jobs has been overwhelmed by a flood of new women workers into predominantly female jobs. In other words, for every woman entering a traditionally male field such as law or auto mechanics, there are several women entering traditional women's fields.

There has been an increasingly vigorous attempt to combat this more subtle form of discrimination—the segregation of women into low-paying occupations—by applying the principle of equal pay for jobs of comparable worth. The argument is that women have been "segregated into job classifications on the basis of sex, and as a result, are paid less than employees in historically predominantly male classifications which require an equivalent [amount] of skill, effort and responsibility." The strategy is to conduct job evaluations, measure the value of different jobs to the employer, and come up with a numerical rating for each. If a secretary is rated the same as a plumber, then both jobs should command the same pay. A score of states and municipalities are under pressure from public employee unions to pay women in low-paying occupations more by applying the principle of comparable worth.

One of the first comparable worth cases was in San Jose, California. In 1981 municipal workers in this city went on strike for nine days to enforce a job evaluation study that demonstrated that certain occupations dominated by women were underpaid. In the end the city provided $1.5 million in pay adjustments to reduce this form of group discrimination.

Another early case was in the private sector. In 1981 the International Union of Electrical Workers (IUE) sued the Westinghouse Corporation for operating with a pay scale that relegated all women workers to the lowest pay grades. The union won, a new job evaluation was undertaken, and women were distributed through the pay scale in a way which reflected the value of the work they did.

Court Ruling

Perhaps the most important legal decision came at the end of 1983, when a federal judge ordered the state of Washington to pay its women workers $800 million in back pay and wage increases on the basis of a comparable worth evaluation. Judge Jack Tanner ruled that the state practiced "direct, overt and institutionalized" discrimination against its women employees. The Washington State ruling triggered scores of cases, and by the end of 1984 litigation was pending across the nation. In numerous states and municipalities public-employee unions are seeking to upset traditional pay patterns that discriminate against women.

Comparable worth has been called the civil rights issue of the 1980s, and it is already a political football—supported by liberals, opposed by conservatives. In the 1984 election campaign it was endorsed by the Mondale-Ferraro ticket and opposed by the Reagan administration. The Democratic leadership of the House of Representatives has endorsed "equal pay for work of comparable social value," while Reagan appointee Clarence M. Pendleton, Jr., chairman of the U.S. Civil Rights Commission, has called comparable worth "the looniest idea since 'Looney Tunes' came on the screen."

Liberals see comparable worth as the best way of producing economic justice for women workers who are shunted into the lowest-paid jobs, and they vigorously defend the use of job evaluations to determine the value of a job. "This is done every day by American business and industry," says Eleanor Holmes Norton, a former head of the Equal Employment Opportunity Commission. As she sees it, "women are doing valuable work which just happens to be underpaid because it is done by women."

"Anti-discrimination efforts are needed if women are to improve their earning power significantly."

Conservative critics respond that unlike the job evaluations of individual companies, which are useful internal measures that take into account the forces of supply and demand, comparable worth plans like the one used in Washington State are not pegged to the market. But many people—including Ray Marshall, economist and secretary of labor in the Carter administration—aren't sure that market forces work with much precision in internal labor markets. "If you compare the predominantly male profession of engineer with the predominantly female profession of nurse, you find there is a shortage of both but the market's response is different. The wages offered to engineers go up while nurses who will work cheap are imported from abroad."

The Cost of Equal Pay

The cost of raising wages for what have traditionally been women's jobs can be high. The Washington State settlement, if upheld by the courts, would cost an estimated $642 million in back pay and $195 million a year in raises. However, in Minnesota the cost of bringing women up to a comparable level with men was only 4 percent of the payroll, a manageable amount. Another issue raised by opponents is that if comparable worth were applied on any scale to private business, it would increase the wage bill and the cost of production, bringing higher prices at home and hindering the ability of American firms to compete in overseas markets.

All this implies that the principle of comparable worth is not going to be accepted quickly or easily in the U.S. labor market.

If occupational segregation is important in explaining the wage gap, the other critical explanatory factor is the heavy load of family responsibilities borne by most working women.

Women attain much less seniority and earn much less money than men whatever occupation they are employed in. As a woman you don't have to be a waitress or a secretary to be badly paid; you don't even have to be discriminated against. You can attend the best professional schools, you can be hired by the most prestigious firms, and you can be treated the same as a man but still find that over a lifetime it is easy to earn a fraction of the amount earned by male contemporaries. The fact is most women bear weighty home and family burdens and need more than equality with men if they are to attain equal earning power in the marketplace....

Need for Support

Both family support measures and antidiscrimination efforts are needed if women are to improve their earning power significantly. In the first place, family support systems are needed so that women can take better advantage of opportunities in the labor market.... If working women had job-protected maternity leave, subsidized day care, and flextime, they would then be better able to seek out high-paying jobs.

Secondly, since women do encounter discrimination in the workplace, vigorous antidiscrimination efforts should continue. Particularly important is the discrimination that ensures low wages for traditional jobs in the pink-collar ghetto.

The bottom line seems to be that working women need more than equal treatment.

Sylvia Ann Hewlett is vice president for economic studies at the United Nations Association.

"'Comparable worth'... must defer to larger questions concerning the kind of families... we want for ourselves and our children."

viewpoint **112**

Comparable Worth Promotes Inequality

Frank Zepezauer

Mary Tyler Moore, television's sweetheart, pushed into Lou Grant's male turf to raise a point. Grant, television's tough guy, wouldn't look up from his papers, but allowed her to argue her case. Then he growled like a grizzly, shuffled his papers, and, without looking up, gave in. His capitulation confirmed stale news. The family wage was dead. And it suggested developing news. So was the family as we knew it.

Mary Tyler Moore's television roles have reflected not only the changing woman but the changing family. She began as Mrs. Dick Van Dyke, the all-American homebody, which image the feminists loved to trash. She returned as a single career woman in her own "Mary Tyler Moore Show" where, as Mary II, she edged forward into the masculine world. Her ambitious but still vulnerable femininity was nevertheless protected by the chivalry she was helping to kill. And now Mary's back, single again after a divorce. Mary III no longer talks to Lou Grant. Now she talks *like* him.

A Scenario

Mary, it seems, is following an agenda, just like the women she represents. Thus her new image, Mary III, connects with the issue of "comparable worth." Where Mary's at suggests where the family's at—or might be very soon. We've argued half a decade about comparable worth: how to measure it, how to pay for it, how to implement it, how to live with it. We've argued mostly about what it will do for women. But we haven't argued as much about what it will do for men, particularly that fading breed called "family men." It's time that we do, time that we ask what comparable worth might do to the family, about what kind of family it might eventually serve.

Frank Zepezauer, "Comparable Worth: Comparable to What?" Reprinted with permission from the September 1986 issue of *Crisis* (PO Box 1006, Notre Dame, IN 46556).

To pick up the trends as reflected in Mary's current agenda, let's return to the opening scene in Lou Grant's office where the family wage was at issue. In this episode Mary II, a television journalist, had won a promotion, only to find it entangled in prejudice. She would replace a man, but she would not earn his salary. She walked diffidently into Lou Grant's office, waited to get his attention, and then asked, very politely, "Why?"

"Because he had a wife and four kids, that's why."

Mary II found it hard to press forward, but she refused to back down.

"Mr. Grant? Uh, Mr. Grant?"

"Yeah!"

"Mr. Grant, uh, I wonder if you might answer just one question?"

"What is it?"

"Do you get paid around here for producing children or producing results?"

Lou Grant's eyes flared. His nostrils twitched. Then he said, "You get the same pay."

"Thank you, Mr. Grant," Mary said sweetly and, as sweetly, departed to tackle her new job.

Score one for Mary's hard-won assertiveness. But recall also that a recently established consensus in the early seventies had helped to build her confidence. In a period when some of us declared that we'd outgrown absolutes, equal pay for equal work had become as absolute as the speed of light. "Equality" as a collective ideal had become as morally energizing as the Holy Grail, the goal toward which we progressed, the standard by which progress was measured, the principle by which standards could be valued.

And yet some of us answered this born-again egalitarianism with stubborn skepticism. I was one of them. I had been living the kind of equality the rest of us apparently wanted. I worked on a gender-balanced high school teaching staff (equality of job distribution). And I shared with others the same salary (equal pay for equal work). On the job a teacher was a teacher was a teacher, and one salary schedule served each, equally.

On the job. That was the problem, then and now. Because *off* the job and at *home,* in the kind of home where my wife and I and our four children were living, an equal pay system created gross inequalities. The same $10,000 I was getting could also support a single teacher or fatten the income of a two-career couple. By several standards applied in those days you could call the gap between my household income and theirs "fair." But you'd have to be wearing ideological blinders if you called it "equal."

No Families

Now, when Mary II, the progressive careerist and evolving woman, arm-twisted her male boss, she had society behind her. Also government. But even though her triumph made a point, it also evaded a point. Mary II, remember, was decidedly single. Many of her show's predicaments developed from the dilemmas of her stubborn independence. And although Mary II often wavered, she always returned to her securely private bachelor pad. At the show's end, Mary II gathered around her all the guys in the office to affirm the workplace kinship the series celebrated. They were Mary's only family, the only one she apparently would ever need.

And for that reason a key question never was asked: If we only worry about producing results in the workplace, what do we do about people who produce children? In my day that answer was, That's your own business; if you choose to have children, you can damn well pay for them. That sentiment carried weight because we were then afraid that the baby boom had generated a population glut. We no longer pinned medals on baby begetters. In fact, we chewed them out. In the media we saw a new hero, a barren patriot, who served the country by foregoing children. Mary II, single and childless, was a TV heroine in more ways than one.

While Mary was evolving, so was the concept of "equality." It once meant equality before the law and equality of opportunity. By that test, my single breadwinning income and six-person household shared the blessing of equality. But by the time Mary II became a hit series, progressives were demanding "equality of results." That development dramatized the question that Lou Grant never asked: Just how will equal pay for equal work *result* in equal households?

If that question was tough to answer in the seventies, try its updated version in the eighties: How will equal pay for *comparable* work result in household equality? To grapple with the swarming complexities of this question, let's invent a scenario for the current Mary Tyler Moore show.

Mary III, you may recall, arrived in the fall of 1985, demonstrating in the first episode that she had grown into one tough lady. She no longer stepped delicately into the boss's chambers. She marched in. She didn't wait for eye-to-eye contact. She demanded it. And if the boss evaded confrontation by clinging to a telephone, she ripped it out of the wall.

In this updated scenario I've invented for her, Mary's new muscular persona orders her boss to give her a pay raise.

"I want 35K a year and I want it now."

"Who says?"

"I say, and the Equity Analysis Associates says, and the Fair Employment Practices Commission says, and the Equal Employment Opportunity Commission says, and the American Federation of Labor says, and the City Board of Supervisors says, and the 10th Circuit Court of Appeals says, and the National Organization of Women says. . . ."

"OK. So that tells me 'who.' Now tell me *what* they're saying."

"That an 'equity study' gives my job 90 points."

"So?"

"How will equal pay for comparable work result in household equality?"

"So, the truck fleet manager also gets 90 points, and *he* earns 35K while *I* earn only 30."

"Maybe I should cut his pay."

"That's your option. All you have to do is explain it to the Teamsters Union."

"Then I'll have to raise all the office salaries. We're talking millions."

"Life is unfair. Capitalism is unfair. Only the FEPC is fair. Now do I get the money or do I rip out your phone again?"

"You get the same pay. Please don't slam the door on the way out."

Move the "woman's agenda" ahead one more notch. "Equality" evolves into "equity" and the cash flow gets rechanneled. But note once more that Mary III, like Mary II, is conspicuously single and childless and that the advanced form of equality she demands still requires a balancing of abstractions. Equal pay for equal work assumed that a worker is a worker is a worker. Comparable pay says a job is a job is a job. Numbers supposedly don't lie, especially when they're joined by equal signs. But people flesh out the numbers and go home to varying households. . . .

Perverse Logic

By some demographic/economic/ideological perversity some . . . women are now pleading for a return of the "family" wage, which means that once again the household circumstances of a worker should be factored into salary determinations. Notice, for example, how one columnist has argued the merits of comparable worth. Having repeated the well known statistics that disclose disparities between male and female majority occupations, she then refers to the minimum requirements for families. "If the poverty guidelines say that a *family of four* needs $9,600 to survive, what about those (mostly female) who make $4,500 as household workers . . . or $7,543 as sales clerks . . . or $9,100 as health service workers?" (My italics and parentheses.) She then asserts that "If working wives and *female heads of household* were paid the same wages that men of similar qualifications earn, about half of the *families* now living in poverty would not be poor." Her solution: higher welfare payments and more comparable work programs.

As the scenario of Mary III illustrates, a woman's private choice to enter the work force, or to have children, generates in turn a *public* obligation. Under a strained interpretation of "equity of results," a woman on the job supposedly needs special compensations to overcome the handicaps of maternity. Only when her company or the government, or both, equalize her circumstances can they supposedly equalize the terms of her employment.

"'Comparable worth' will benefit some people. . . .But those people . . . are not the only ones worth considering."

That's just fine for women who choose to enter the work force, but not so good for women who choose to stay at home and not so good for the men who support them. The key word here is "choice" and the key consideration is "limited duration." The full-time homemaker, the traditional housewife, is by most accounts, a dying breed. But not the temporary homemaker who stays with her children for five or ten years until she can return to her career. She's not only *not* dying; she's in fact gaining new life, and adding new constituents to her cause. That puts her and her husband in direct confrontation with the dogmatic full-time female careerist.

The political power of the housewife constituency, full or part-time, has figured prominently in the theories of utopian egalitarians. The housewife must go, they say, if not by force of circumstance, then by the force of persuasion. Or coercion.

Some theorists see the latter as an unavoidable price of ultimate equality. Listen to one of them speaking to a 1978 Status of Women seminar at Stanford University. In answer to a question whether some women should be permitted the "option" of staying at home, she declared that such choices

threatened equality because if only 20 percent of women stayed home the rest would have "to pay the price of deviance." If laggards still harbor counter-revolutionary sentiments, then according to Karen DeCrow, another theorist, they should not only be "permitted and encouraged" to reshape the economics of their lives, but also "forced." . . .

Yet people like Karen DeCrow would like us to go further. She knows—the first feminists knew, all radical feminists know—that the only way to achieve equality between the sexes is to assume that only individuals matter and that only salaried public work is worthwhile. That means that private "parenting," the last vestige of bourgeois sentimentality, must become a state monopoly. Such a vision was always implicit in the contemporary woman's movement. When feminists demanded "fifty-fifty across the board," complete parity between the sexes at work and at home, they knew there was only one way to achieve it. The private family had to go.

Larger Questions

But, in our blessedly pluralistic society, not all individuals share the feminist faith. Thus "comparable worth," touted as the decade's hottest issue, must defer to larger questions concerning the kind of families and the kind of communities we want for ourselves and our children. Such questions have been clouded by a modernist prejudice which assumes that all family traditionalists worship in Jerry Falwell's church. But wherever you find yourself on the religio/philosophical spectrum, you will still have to confront questions about "the family" and ask, in fact, whether we should continue to speak of "the" family as normative.

No doubt "comparable worth" will benefit some people. It will also meet certain definitions of equality. But those people and that definition are not the only ones worth considering. Others deserve our attention. Equally.

Frank Zepezauer is a freelance writer and a public school teacher.

"The Family and Medical Leave Act is needed . . . to address the new realities of working parents."

The Parental Leave Law Is Economically Necessary

William Clay, Patricia Schroeder, and Christopher Dodd

The United States is in the midst of a demographic revolution. Demographic changes are altering the American workforce, as well as the American family.

Today, 60 percent of women with children aged three to five years are in the workforce. They represent the fastest growing segment of the U.S. workforce. Almost half of all mothers with children under the age of one are working outside the home.

The majority of women work because of economic need. Over half of the 45.6 million children in two parent families have both parents in the workforce. According to the most current data, 40 percent of married working women have husbands who earn less than $15,000.

The once typical American family, where father worked outside the home while mother stayed at home with the kids, is vanishing. The majority of American parents are two-earner couples working outside the home.

There currently exists no federal policy addressing these changes in the American workforce and family. The lack of employment policies which deal with working parents forces many individuals to choose between job security and parenting. Job security is an issue not only for working parents planning a family, but also for workers who may become temporarily disabled due to pregnancy, accident, or other nonoccupational reasons.

Current law defines discrimination on the basis of pregnancy as sex discrimination. This law, the Pregnancy Discrimination Act, requires that pregnancy-related health conditions be treated like other short-term serious health conditions.

Unfortunately, current federal law does not require employers to offer temporary medical leave for *any* employee for *any* reason. Every year many workers become sick or suffer accidents away from their jobs and cannot work for temporary periods ranging from a few weeks to several months. There is no uniform policy that provides reasonable job security for these workers.

Poor Job Protection

In 1983, the Social Security Administration estimated that among the 91.6 million wage earners in this country, only 59.1 million or 64% were covered by a formal temporary disability plan. These formal plans offer varying degrees of wage replacement. Many, however, do not offer job protection.

The Family and Medical Leave Act proposes a national leave policy that provides job-protected leave for workers to meet parental responsibilities, and to deal with serious health conditions.

The bill would provide parents with four months of unpaid job-protected leave to care for a newborn, newly-adopted, or seriously ill child. In addition, the House bill would provide family leave for up to four months for employees with seriously ill parents. The Family and Medical Leave Act would also provide all workers with a six month unpaid leave for any serious illness that prevents them from working.

Despite the increasing number of company-sponsored family leave policies, at least 60% of women employed have no paid maternity related benefits that permit a six-week leave—the minimum recuperation period prescribed by obstetricians.

According to one national survey, just half of large employers offer unpaid but job-protected childcare leave for women after childbirth. Paternity leaves allowed by large employers are generally limited to a few days, according to another study.

Small companies, while creating the largest percentage of new jobs, have been found to be least likely to provide employee benefits such as sick leave, pension coverage, health insurance, or

The Congressional Staffs of Representatives William Clay, Patricia Schroeder, and Senator Christopher Dodd, "The Family and Medical Leave Act," a briefing paper, February 3, 1987.

Maternity and Parental Leave Policies: A Comparative View

Country	Duration	Job Security	Salary/Duration	Recipient
Canada	17-41 Weeks	Yes	60%/15 Weeks	Mother
Italy	22-48 Weeks	Yes	80%/22 Weeks	Mother
Germany	14-26 Weeks	Yes	100%/14-18 Weeks	Mother
Sweden	12-52 Weeks	Yes	90%/38 Weeks	Mother or Father
Finland	35 Weeks	Yes	100%/35 Weeks	Mother or Father
Austria	16-52 Weeks	Yes	100%/20 Weeks	Mother
Chile	18 Weeks	Yes	100%/18 Weeks	Unspecified
USA*	0	0	0	0

*No Federal Policy

Source: Women at Work, ILO Global Survey, 1984; Kamerman, Maternity & Parental Benefits & Leave, 1980.

disability benefits.

The January 13, 1987 Supreme Court decision in *California Savings and Loan Association v. Guerra* has given heightened impetus to the national effort to enact family and medical leave legislation. The Court found that the California law granting job-protected maternity leave for up to four months to temporarily disabled pregnant workers does not conflict with the Pregnancy Discrimination Act amendments to Title VII of the Civil Rights Act.

Social and Economic Realities

The Family and Medical Leave Act is needed to respond to the ad hoc policies of state maternity leave legislation, and to address the new realities of working parents. Both mothers and fathers will be able to take a period of leave from their jobs in order to participate in the early care of newborn or newly-adopted children or to attend to a son, daughter, mother, or father with a serious health condition.

Futhermore, the Family and Medical Leave Act will provide job protection for all workers, assuring them that if they are struck by a sudden illness or if they have a temporarily disabling accident, they will be able to return to their jobs.

The Family and Medical Leave Act is a positive response to a demographic revolution and the important social and economic realities which underpin it.

The Subcommittee on Civil Service, chaired by Representative Patricia Schroeder, sent a questionnaire on parental leave policies and practices to 58 executive agencies on August 21, 1985. Fifty-three agencies responded.

Analysis of the responses reveals that, although no official government-wide policy exists, the practices of most agencies are remarkably similar: if there is any leave offered at all, it is done at the discretion of each individual supervisor. This results in a widely disparate range of leave permitted from

agency to agency and even within the same agency.

The Office of Personnel Management (OPM) has issued guidelines on maternity benefits. There is no separate statutory "maternity" leave category in the federal government. Any absence for maternity is to be taken as sick leave, annual leave, or leave without pay.

The federal government treats pregnancy like any other medically certified temporary disability. Therefore, sick leave may only be used to cover the time required for physical examinations and to cover the period of incapacitation. A woman may take any sick leave she had accrued. In some instances, agencies will advance sick leave; many, however, do not.

If a mother wishes to take additional leave after the baby's birth, she may request any annual leave she has earned or a leave without pay. Agencies are not required to grant either of these.

Fathers and parents adopting children are not entitled to sick leave. They must rely on their supervisors agreeing to their taking earned annual leave or leave without pay.

Some agencies have developed leave policy statements. Others have collective bargaining agreements providing specific maternity or parental leave benefits. Yet, all 53 agencies responding leave the final decisions involving maternity, paternity and adoption leave up to the discretion of the supervisor.

The Family and Medical Leave Act

The following is a summary of the Family and Medical Leave Act. Provisions are included in both the House and Senate bills unless otherwise stated.

Definitions: Employee—The House bill covers all employees employed for 3 consecutive months or 500 hours, whichever occurs earlier. The Senate bill covers all full time and permanent, part-time employees.

Employer—covers employers with 15 or more employees.

Unpaid Family Leave: An employee may take up to 18 weeks of leave over a 24 month period upon the birth or adoption or serious health condition of a child. The House bill also permits employees to take family leave to care for a seriously ill parent.

Leave may be taken on a reduced hour basis, not to exceed 36 work weeks, and scheduled so as not to unduly disrupt the employer's operations.

An employee may substitute appropriate paid leave for part of the unpaid leave. The House bill also allows an employer to require the substitution of other appropriate paid leave.

Under the House bill:
- leave must be taken within 1 year of birth or placement of a child,
- employees are required to provide reasonable notice if possible, and
- employees must schedule their leave to accommodate the needs of the employer, if the need for leave is foreseeable and it is medically feasible to do so.

Unpaid Medical Leave: An employee may take up to 26 weeks of leave over a 12 month period when unable to perform his or her job due to a serious health condition.

The employee may substitute appropriate paid leave for part of the unpaid leave. The House bill also permits the employer to require the substitution of appropriate paid leave.

Employers may require medical certification.

Under the House bill, an employee shall provide reasonable notice if possible. The House bill also requires that employees schedule leave to accommodate the employer, if the need for leave is foreseeable and it is medically feasible to do so.

"The Family and Medical Leave Act is a positive response to a demographic revolution."

Employment and Benefits Protection: Upon returning to work, the employee is to be restored to his or her previous job or to an equivalent position.

Under the House bill, an employer may limit an employee's combined family and medical leave to 36 weeks over a one year period.

During the leave period, the employer must continue health benefit coverage on the same basis as prior to the leave.

Enforcement: Both civil and administrative enforcement is provided.

Remedies for violation include reinstatement, backpay and benefits and consequential damages.

Representative William Clay, Representative Patricia Schroeder, and Senator William Dodd sponsored the federal Family and Medical Leave Act in Congress.

The Parental Leave Law Is Unnecessary

Allan C. Carlson

"An idea whose time has come," Colorado Representative Pat Schroeder calls it. A true "pro-family issue," says a representative of the United States Catholic Conference. A matter of simple justice, the National Organization of Women (NOW) insists.

The issue is parental leave, a proposed Federal law that would require employers to grant extended leaves of absence to female and *male* employees for purposes of childbirth or child care. Advocates note that the fastest growing segment of the workforce is found among mothers with children under the age of three. Eighty percent of all employed women become pregnant at some point in their working lives, and over half of them will be back to work within a year after childbirth. America, they say, must adjust to these sweeping changes.

In fact, though, the logic behind mandated parental leave is often murky, if not schizophrenic. Moreover, the demand for universal parental leave actually rises out of the ideological contradictions of modern feminism, which translate into calls for radical social reconstruction and massive expansion of the American welfare state.

The Maternity Question

Most recent students of family policy, it is true, lambast the United States for its institutional backwardness on the maternity question. For example, panels of business executives, labor leaders, and child-care specialists at Yale University and the Economic Policy Council have lamented American nonrecognition of parenthood and recommended that job-protected leaves of six months, with partial pay, be made available to all new parents.

Sociologists Sheila Kamerman and Alfred Kahn note that 70 nations, including every major industrial nation except the United States, provide paid maternity or parental leaves through national legislation. Sweden, for example, grants 12 months of leave, at 90 percent of the maximum insured wage. Canada covers 60 percent of the insured wage for a maximum of 17 weeks. Yet in the USA, Kamerman and Kahn add, a "real revolution in family life styles" symbolized by the working mother has produced no major policy changes. Under the terms of the Pregnancy Disability Amendment of 1978, firms with disability benefits are only required to treat pregnancy as they treat any other disability. Kamerman and Kahn complain that, in this mode, pregnancy and birth are defined as illnesses, rather than maternity, while employees at firms without disability policies lose coverage altogether. American attitudes have been "strangely unaccommodating" to maternal policies, they conclude. The "larger meaning of maternity as motherhood has been ignored."

Writing in *American Psychologist*, two Yale scholars complain that the United States gives "no recognition" to the fact that a healthy parent may have a psychological need for some time off with a new baby or that both parent and infant could benefit "from a six-month get-acquainted period." They cry out: "How have we come to such an impasse, where mothers and fathers must be in the workforce, psychologically safe day care is prohibitively expensive, and yet there is no funding to help either parent stay home for even a few months to take care of a baby?"

The popular press has fallen behind the call for action. *U.S. News & World Report* says that "companies preach family values, but in most cases their practices do little to ease work-family strains." *Glamour* complains that "there is no national policy to protect women's interests." *Ms.* notes bitterly that few companies have facilities which allow mothers to pump and store breastmilk. *Working Woman* adds

Allan C. Carlson, "Working Mothers at Home: The Cultural Politics of the Parental Leave Debate," *Persuasion at Work*, October 1986. Reprinted with permission.

that companies also abuse adopting parents and concludes: "Are we pushing women out of the work force and back home because there are no systems out there to help them with their families?" . . .

Two-Career Households

Congress has listened and responded [with] the "Family and Medical Leave Act of 1986." . . .

The bill cites the growing number of single-parent and two-career households in America and the importance "for the development of the child and the family unit that fathers and mothers be able to participate in early child rearing." It says that many working parents are forced to choose between job security and parenting and declares its purpose to be the balancing of "the demands of the workplace with the needs of families." The committee-approved measure would require all companies with over 14 employees to allow men and women up to 18 weeks of unpaid leave from their work after the birth or adoption of a child, or in order to care for a sick child or parent. Employees exercising this new right must be guaranteed their old, equivalent, or better job on their return, as well as full benefit coverage during the leave and seniority privileges. Significantly, the measure would also create a Commission on Paid Parental and Medical Leave, instructed to study and recommend steps toward creating a comprehensive "system of salary replacement" like those found in other industrialized countries.

"Government should not mandate one approach to benefits for all companies."

Opposition to the bill comes primarily from the U.S. Chamber of Commerce and small business groups. They argue that government should not mandate one approach to benefits for all companies. Most large companies already provide maternity leave, they note. Ninety-five percent of the Fortune 500 companies offer an average of eight weeks of disability, including cash benefits and job protection. A majority of firms either now provide or are considering paid personal days for child care and family matters as an additional benefit. The financial impact of this measure, they conclude, would primarily strike small firms without the resources to hire and train part-time replacements for the leave period.

These groups rallied around a substitute measure, proposed by Republican Representative Marge Roukema of New Jersey. While agreeing with the liberal majority that the "time is now at hand to develop a pro-working-family leave policy," she proposed alternate language that would have reduced the leave period, increased the number of

exempted employers, and scuttled the commission on paid leave.

The effort failed, though, as the proponents of the more comprehensive measure successfully held the pro-family ground. Indeed, in the pregnancy bill debate, liberals are beginning to rediscover the power of the *family* and *motherhood* labels as levers for social reform, while the conservative opposition has been left with arguments based on utility and efficiency and consequently doing what, until five years ago, conservatives usually did best: lose slowly.

Theoretical Schizophrenia

Unfortunately, emotions surrounding *home, hearth,* and *babies* have obscured the larger questions. Indeed, close analysis of the parental leave concept reveals great mental confusion masking a strongly ideological agenda.

This almost pathological illogic is apparent in the volume frequently cited as best presenting the social and intellectual case for the plan. In *Maternity Policies and Working Women,* Kamerman, Kahn, and Paul Kingston mobilize all the arguments noted above for a Federal law, but are strangely ambivalent about the actual need for parental care. They note with some satisfaction, for example, that the fertility rate for American women has fallen dramatically. Wives aged 18 to 34, for example, have borne an average of only 1.5 children, with employed women moving toward a one-child norm. This trend toward depopulation, they happily note, "makes the costs of providing maternity benefits both more predictable and less costly."

The authors also strain to emphasize that parents are not actually all that important. The research, they say, "does not suggest that mothers cannot safely be members of the labor force or plan on use of child care programs." Day care, even from the earliest period after birth, is perfectly fine for mother and baby, so long as it is freely chosen. In line with this, Kamerman and friends decry the wearisome American emphasis on "matters other than maternity benefit," such as "the possible negative effects on children caused by absence of working mothers from the home," the negative impact of two-earner households on the living standard of one-earner families, or "the alleged effects of maternal employment on family stress and family break-up." These are nonissues, they say, distracting the nation from the critical need for social reconstruction.

At the same time, the researchers use carefully chosen words to transform what they have first labeled a nonnecessity and a pure matter of choice into a right so compelling as to require the full backing of Federal law. They begin: "When individual resources or social policy can make it possible, it is a good strategy to ensure a joint child-parent start for a period of at least three to nine months, even though parental circumstances might then require labor force participation of both parents, or a single parent, and alternative child care arrangements." A few pages later, this extremely cautious affirmation of a "bonding" period for mother—or father—and baby is translated into semihysterical assaults on the American system, as in: "Don't we value children and understand optimal conditions for child development in the early months of life?" Somewhat later, the same bonding period is redefined as the very heart of the American polity, as they conclude: "Maternity policy is integral to our [nation's] core values and ideology."

A Twisted Message

The mind-twisting message that the "mother-at-home is not important and the Federal government must therefore force all employers to grant parental leaves" pervades the popular women's press, too. *Glamour*, for example, stresses the absolute moral imperative for parental leave as national policy. Yet the magazine also encourages new mothers to get back to work as quickly as possible, warning darkly that "babies are hard to resist once they're at this stage [one to six months], and mothers can sometimes find it difficult to 'break away' if they delay too long." It adds that no matter when mothers go back to work, "there is no evidence that exclusive mothering is good for babies." *Glamour* also reports on the personal triumph of one Washington, DC, radio newscaster who did manage to leave her newborn and "loved it": "On the first day back, my sitter brought the baby in so I could nurse him. I was working and saw a stroller out of the corner of my eye. I thought, 'Who's that baby?' I was so into a work mode that I forgot for four hours that I had a baby."

What accounts for such disjointed thought? Simply put, we see here the frantic efforts of ideologues to piece back together a social order at least capable of its own reproduction, after the dissolution of the natural bonds and economic structure of the old American family system.

Parental leave was never before an American issue because, until about 1965, the nation's family and economic systems meshed relatively well. Men were expected to marry and to work, to be "good providers," to set a good table, to pay the mortgage, to buy the shoes, to contribute to the church, and to keep their children warmly clothed. Through a variety of formal and informal devices, the working father generally received a "family wage" sufficient to support his dependents. Women were expected to marry and to care full-time for the resulting offspring. If they worked before marriage, they received pay calculated on an "individual" basis and were expected to resign on the wedding day or, later, on becoming pregnant. In 1930, for example, 77 percent of American school systems still

refused to hire married women, while 63 percent automatically dismissed teachers on their marriage. As late as the mid-1960's, a hefty 87 percent of American housewives saw "bread-winning" as their husband's primary role. In 1980, though, the Census Bureau provided a benchmark of change, deciding that year that it would no longer automatically denominate the male as a family's head of household.

Of course, that social and moral order constructed so as to reinforce marriage and the birth of children has now vanished from public view. Many millions of Americans still live by its tenets, but they find themselves strangers in a strange land. . . .

Even as a utilitarian response, though, is "parental leave" the way to go? When one actually looks at the differential or discriminatory impact of the currently favored plan, the answer is no. As in all state-mandated benefits, there would be winners and losers, and the losers under the parental leave plan would be fairly numerous.

Who Will Pay?

Who would bear the negative costs for this attempt at social reconstruction? There appear to be four groups:

Small businesses. Large companies with employees numbering in the thousands find it relatively easy to cover a four-month vacancy caused by a parental leave through the use of similarly trained personnel. Small companies have much less flexibility and would commonly face great problems of filling a skilled vacancy with short-term help. The real, if somewhat invisible, costs of providing leave would also have to come out of some other pocket, possibly through a reduction in other benefits or in a greater reluctance, at the margins, to hire new employees.

"The losers under the parental leave plan would be fairly numerous."

Lower income families. An unpaid leave of absence is tailored primarily to the needs of highly paid, professional women who can afford more easily a period of time without income. The working poor and families at the lower end of the income scale have less "choice" here and receive a "benefit" that they cannot afford, while probably losing other benefits that employers might have offered.

Traditional families. Behind all the hype about the massive flow of mothers into the labor force lurks one little-noticed fact: nearly half of mothers with children age three and younger are *not* in the labor force. About the same proportion do not return to work after their first child's birth; they become a clear majority of mothers after the second and third births. Often at considerable personal and professional sacrifice, these women continue to perform the socially valuable task of nurturing small children on a full-time basis. The "opportunity cost" (foregone income) of this choice is, on average, nearly $16,000 a year. It is unclear why this financial sacrifice for family-supportive ends should receive no recognition from the government, while working mothers demand benefits for which others (small businesses, the poor, the traditional) will directly or indirectly pay. One possible response is that leaves should be transformed into a government maternity grant, paid to all mothers, whether working or not. While plausible, the answer simply reveals how partial measures, in face of the equity problem, quickly descend down the welfare state's slippery slope.

"Parental leave should be left as a voluntary option for firms seeking to attract those employees who choose to model their lives on that arrangement."

Children. Common sense tells us that an ideological vision, however fine in theory, cannot turn women into fathers or men into mothers. Social research, fortunately, confirms the same point and suggests that efforts to create the envisioned "new human type" are futile and can only damage the children. A team of research psychologists headed by Michael Lamb set out in 1980 to determine whether "nontraditional" Swedish fathers, who, under various state pressures, had taken parental leave to care full time for their infant children, were as effective as stay-at-home mothers and more effective than "traditional" fathers who worked. Measuring qualitative actions such as discipline, play, and affection, the team hypothesized that a reversal in sex roles and the assumption of "the primary caretaker role" by the father would result in an effectively nurturing, unisex parent.

To their surprise, though, they found that mothers—whether working or at home—proved more likely to hold, tend, vocalize to, smile at, and display affection toward their infants than did fathers, whether traditional or "caretaking." Moreover, they discovered that while traditional mothers engaged in more effective play with infants than working mothers, the opposite effect occurred among men: traditional "working" fathers engaged in better play with their infants than "nontraditional" fathers. In other words, men did not change even after being the full-time caretaking parent; in some ways, in fact, they became less effective.

In sum, women remained better mothers; men

remained better fathers; and social engineering had failed. The researchers reluctantly concluded that biological gender was apparently "a more important influence on parental behavior than caretaking role or sex role." They did, though, hold out hope that truly "radical changes in gender-related prescriptions and expectations" might still make a difference. In the interim, though, it was clear that infants made by the social engineers to suffer the full-time caretaking of their fathers were paying the price of stunted psychological and emotional development.

The Alternative

What, then, is the alternative to parental leave? Back to the old model where Dad worked and Mom stayed at home? While that system had more logic to it than is usually granted, it does not represent a viable policy option. . . .

Rather, we should cease trying to repair a symptom of a problem and focus instead on the problem itself: the collapse of the historic family-wage economy in the United States and our failure to acknowledge or correct the situation. By 1976, only 40 percent of American jobs paid enough to support a family of five in minimal comfort, not so long ago the standard measure of a fair wage. Today, the figure is closer to 25 percent. Particularly on the lower and low-middle sectors of the income scale, there is truth to the cry of women and men that two incomes are needed just to get along. We know, for example, that perceived "income inadequacy" is tied heavily to employment in the "service sector," where the large majority of new female workers is concentrated. The inflationary economy of the 1969-1983 period also masked a general stagnation of real household income, where a family's standard-of-living could be maintained only by sending a second (or third) earner into the workforce and/or by reducing household size through the avoidance of children.

Finally, as George Gilder has pointed out, it is a great mistake to view "working women" as a uniform mass of full-time laborers. In 1984, only 37 percent of all women ages 20 to 64 held full-time, year-round jobs (including teaching). The large majority were either homemakers or holding seasonal or part-time work. Even managerial, professional, and executive women—by a 51 to 19 percent margin—still prefer seasonal or part-time to full-time work, if they can find it. A parental leave policy constructed to help meet an ideological vision of dubious, if not absurd, dimensions and catering primarily to the needs of the richest segment of the target population does almost nothing to accommodate this great complexity.

The family-wage problem and the real diversity of family working arrangements can both be addressed, though, through a "supply-side" family policy, allowing parents to keep more of their earned income through tax deductions and credits keyed to birth, age, and number of children. The components of such a plan could include: (1) raising the personal exemption, for children only, to $4,000 per child; (2) granting an indexed, $500 child-care tax credit to every family for each dependent preschool child, up to a maximum of $1,000 (at present, the credit is available only to parents who hire someone else to care for their children); (3) grant an indexed, refundable $500 income-tax credit for each dependent child, up to the taxpayer's and employer's FICA or payroll tax; and (4) grant an additional, refundable $500 credit in the year of a child's birth or adoption, with the same ceiling.

Support the Family

This approach recognizes the contribution to society that women and men make through the birth of a child and allows parents to retain more of their earned income when they need it the most. It gives meaningful social recognition to motherhood without discriminating against either working mothers or those engaged in full-time child care. It provides real financial relief to families, without making them dependent on the state or increasing the size of government (indeed, these measures would work to reduce the size of government). It restores a form of a family wage that is far more efficient than the pre-1965 model and that does not rest on institutionalized discrimination. It accommodates all forms of family and work arrangements and discriminates against none. The sole value judgment behind this plan is that children have social value, which merits recognition.

Parental leave should be left as a voluntary option for firms seeking to attract those employees who choose to model their lives on that arrangement. Yet that life choice should not be forced by law on all Americans. As a universal prescription, its origins are blatantly ideological. Its deeper intent is to help impose a new and twisted model of human nature through the coercive magic of social engineering. Accordingly, it is inappropriate to a free society.

Allan C. Carlson edits Persuasion at Work *and is the executive vice president of The Rockford Institute.*

"The Supreme Court explicitly ruled that women as well as blacks and other minorities can receive preferential treatment."

Johnson v. Santa Clara County: An Overview

Richard Stengel

After four gritty years working on the road for the Santa Clara County transportation agency—patching holes, shoveling asphalt, opening culverts—Diane Joyce applied in 1980 for a less strenuous desk job as a road dispatcher. At the time not one of the California agency's 238 skilled positions was held by a woman. Joyce knew, however, that two years earlier the county had enacted a voluntary affirmative-action policy designed to correct that imbalance.

Paul Johnson, a white male who had worked for the agency for 13 years, also applied. He and Joyce were among the seven applicants who scored above 70 on the oral exam and were considered qualified. Joyce scored 73, Johnson 75. The local supervisor picked Johnson, but the county's affirmative-action coordinator recommended Joyce. When she got the job, Johnson got a lawyer. Like Allen Bakke and Brian Weber and countless other white males since the advent of affirmative-action programs some 20 years ago, Johnson claimed he was a victim of reverse discrimination.

In its most significant affirmative-action decision since the murky resolution of Bakke's case against the University of California in 1978, the Supreme Court ruled 6 to 3 that it was permissible for the Santa Clara agency to take sex and race into account in employment decisions. "I'm very proud," said Joyce. "I've waited a long time for this." Said Johnson, who is now retired and lives in Washington State: "I'm shocked and disappointed. A ruling like this will cause prejudice in people who have never been prejudiced before."

After nearly a decade of on-the-one-hand, on-the-other-hand rulings, [the] decision provides the clearest declaration yet on the role of affirmative

action as a remedy for inequality in the American workplace. For the first time the Supreme Court explicitly ruled that women as well as blacks and other minorities can receive preferential treatment. Even more significantly, the decision endorsed a voluntary affirmative-action plan in a situation where there was no proven history of discrimination; all that was necessary, wrote Justice William Brennan for the majority, was evidence of a "manifest imbalance" in the number of women or minorities holding the positions in question.

The decision affects the most universal of employment situations in America: workplaces where it is hard to prove past discrimination but where there is a statistical shortage of women and minorities in certain positions. It is the strongest link in a chain of decisions suggesting that voluntary affirmative-action programs are a desirable way to right such imbalances.

The ruling, predictably enough, delighted civil rights and women's groups while angering the Reagan Administration and others who have been waging an ardent crusade to roll back affirmative action. Many business groups applauded the decision because it helped clarify the legal status of voluntary programs and is likely to discourage future reverse-discrimination actions.

Johnson's suit was based on Title VII of the 1964 Civil Rights Act, which makes it unlawful for an employer "to deprive any individual of employment opportunities or otherwise adversely affect his status as an employee because of such individual's race, color, religion, sex or national origin." Brennan's opinion was guided by the court's 1979 *Weber* ruling upholding an apprentice program in a Kaiser Aluminum plant in Gramercy, La., that reserved 50% of the slots for blacks. Brennan concluded that the Santa Clara plan was "consistent with Title VII's purpose of eliminating the effects of employment discrimination." He wrote, "Given the obvious

Richard Stengel, "Balancing Act," *Time*, April 6, 1987. Copyright 1987 Time Inc. All rights reserved. Reprinted with the permission of TIME.

america's economy/65

imbalance in the skilled craft division and given the agency's commitment to eliminating such imbalances . . . it was appropriate to consider as one fact the sex of Ms. Joyce in making its decision."

The Santa Clara program, which set a temporary "goal" of filling 36% of its skilled jobs with women, was an attempt to achieve a "work force that mirrored in its major job classification the percentage of women in the area labor market." Brennan argued that the plan, like that in *Weber*, did not "unnecessarily trammel" the interests of whites by creating an absolute bar to their employment.

In a blistering and forceful dissent, Justice Antonin Scalia wrote that the decision "effectively requires employers, public as well as private, to engage in intentional discrimination on the basis of race or sex." He was particularly critical of the decision to permit statistical imbalances to be criteria for justifying an affirmative-action program rather than requiring there be evidence of past discrimination. "This is an enormous expansion, undertaken without the slightest justification or analysis."

"The Johnson decision, employers believe, protects their affirmative action programs from reverse-discrimination suits."

The ruling, Scalia contended, turns Title VII on its head. "The court today completes the process of converting [Title VII] from a guarantee that race or sex will not be the basis for employment determinations, to a guarantee that it often will. Ever so subtly . . . we effectively replace the goal of a discrimination-free society with the quite incompatible goal of proportionate representation by race and by sex in the workplace."

After hearing of the court's decision, President Reagan, who has long maintained that affirmative action is immoral and illegal, said simply, "Obviously, I disagree." From the outset, the Administration has vigorously sought to reverse the course of affirmative action, insisting that hiring goals are the same as illegal quotas. The court has now completely rebuffed that effort. Some observers suggest that the Administration's heavy-handed attempts to dismantle affirmative action may have backfired and pushed the court to assert its position more forcefully.

The difficult and divisive national debate over affirmative action arises from a philosophical tension between two basic American values: the protection of individual rights and the quest for social equality. Opponents of affirmative action argue that each individual has the right to be judged on merit.

Setting special standards for blacks or women, they maintain, is demeaning and ultimately destructive, both to society and to those who are the intended beneficiaries. Some prominent blacks and women agree, on the grounds that affirmative action is condescending and leads its beneficiaries to call their own achievements into question.

Proponents of affirmative action contend that equality for all can be achieved only through temporary preferences given to blacks, women and other groups that have historically suffered discrimination. It is perverse, they argue, to use civil rights laws to block the very goals—better opportunities for blacks and women—those laws were intended to further.

Preferential treatment in employment was first mandated by Lyndon Johnson in a 1965 presidential order stating that companies doing business with the Government were required to take "affirmative action" to hire women and minorities. Thousands of private companies followed suit, many of them on the grounds that it was good for business. Since then, affirmative action has helped change the way America does business: the Bureau of Labor Statistics projects that between 1985 and 1995, blacks and women will account for three-fourths of all labor-force growth.

The Johnson decision, employers believe, protects their affirmative-action programs from reverse-discrimination suits. "This decision wipes away the last lingering doubts," says James McDaniel, manager of affirmative action at E.I. duPont. "Employers can now statistically correct imbalances without the fear of frivolous challenges." In the past, employers with affirmative-action programs had to worry about disgruntled whites as well as excluded minorities. Notes John Jacob, president of the National Urban League: "I have had companies say to me that they intended to go ahead with affirmative-action programs but were concerned about the mounting litigation brought by white males." While the ruling insulates business from reverse-discrimination suits, it may make them more vulnerable to discrimination claims on the part of women and minorities.

Many women judged the decision to be properly tough. "I've always said that affirmative action has to hurt a little," says Stanford Law Professor Barbara Babcock. "This is a decision that hurts." Women's groups saw the ruling as a way of helping them penetrate job markets traditionally sealed off from women. Says Claudia Withers, a staff attorney at the Women's Legal Defense Fund in Washington: "As women see opportunities open, they will apply for jobs where before they felt unwelcome." The decision appears particularly relevant to jobs that require no specialized training—blue-collar employment where most applicants, whether female, black, white or male, are generally on an equal footing.

Conservatives regarded the decision as another example of the state's infringing on individual liberties and a retreat from the goal of a truly gender-neutral, color-blind society. Michael McDonald, president of the conservative Washington Legal Foundation, says the plan endorsed by the court "was social engineering on a scale I have yet to see equaled elsewhere. Every special-interest group was awarded the right to a job." Some saw the decision as camouflage for quotas. "It is exactly what civil rights law was designed to free us of," declared Nathan Perlmutter, executive director of the Anti-Defamation League. "I consider performance based on race, color, creed or sex, in the absence of evidence that the person has been discriminated against, to be a form of well-intended but nonetheless mischievous discrimination."

"The Johnson case will almost certainly result in more affirmative-action programs."

Not all businessmen regarded the ruling as a benison. Many employers feel handcuffed by affirmative action and fret that the latest ruling establishes an even more difficult standard for them to follow. "The Supreme Court has changed the ground rules," says Richard Bradley, vice president of the Merchants and Manufacturers Association, a Los Angeles-based organization with 3,206 members. "Now they're saying unless you lean toward a protected category, you may be committing a discriminatory act."

The Johnson case will almost certainly result in more affirmative-action programs on the part of employers. Julius Chambers, director of the NAACP Legal Defense Fund, suggests the ruling will "invite" organizations pushing for affirmative action for women and minorities to persuade employers to enact plans to redress any imbalances in their work force. Says Chambers: "There is less basis for an employer responding that it can't because of the uncertainty of the law." Now, after years of judicial uncertainty on affirmative action, future court decisions are likely to concern the limits on specific plans rather than the validity of the concept.

Richard Stengel is a staff writer for Time.

The Supreme Court Made the Right Decision in *Johnson*

John Paul Stevens

Editor's note: The following viewpoint is the concurring opinion of Justice John Paul Stevens on the Supreme Court's March 25, 1987 ruling in Paul E. Johnson v. The Transportation Agency of Santa Clara County, California.

While I join the Court's opinion, I write separately to explain my view of this case's position in our evolving antidiscrimination law and to emphasize that the opinion does not establish the permissible outer limits of voluntary programs undertaken by employers to benefit disadvantaged groups.

Antidiscrimination measures may benefit protected groups in two distinct ways. As a sword, such measures may confer benefits by specifying that a person's membership in a disadvantaged group must be a neutral, irrelevant factor in governmental or private decisionmaking or, alternatively, by compelling decisionmakers to give favorable consideration to disadvantaged group status. As a shield, an antidiscrimination statute can also help a member of a protected class by assuring decisionmakers in some instances that, when they elect for good reasons of their own to grant a preference of some sort to a minority citizen, they will not violate the law. The Court properly holds that the statutory shield allowed respondent to take Diane Joyce's sex into account in promoting her to the road dispatcher position.

A New Interpretation

Prior to 1978 the Court construed the Civil Rights Act of 1964 as an absolute blanket prohibition against discrimination which neither required nor permitted discriminatory preferences for any group, minority or majority. The Court unambiguously endorsed the neutral approach, first in the context of

John Paul Stevens, concurring opinion of the Supreme Court in the case of Paul E. Johnson, petitioner v. Transportation Agency, Santa Clara County, California, March 25, 1987.

gender discrimination and then in the context of racial discrimination against a white person. As I explained in my separate opinion in *University of California Regents* v. *Bakke,* Congress intended "'to eliminate all practices which operate to disadvantage the employment opportunities of any group protected by Title VII including Caucasians.'" If the Court had adhered to that construction of the Act, petitioner would unquestionably prevail in this case. But it has not done so.

In the *Bakke* case in 1978 and again in *Steelworkers* v. *Weber,* (1979), a majority of the Court interpreted the antidiscriminatory strategy of the statute in a fundamentally different way. The Court held in the *Weber* case that an employer's program designed to increase the number of black craftworkers in an aluminum plant did not violate Title VII. It remains clear that the Act does not *require* any employer to grant preferential treatment on the basis of race or gender, but since 1978 the Court has unambiguously interpreted the statute to *permit* the voluntary adoption of special programs to benefit members of the minority groups for whose protection the statute was enacted. Neither the "same standards" language used in *McDonald,* nor the "color-blind" rhetoric used by the Senators and Congressmen who enacted the bill, is now controlling. Thus, the only problem for me is whether to adhere to an authoritative construction of the Act that is at odds with my understanding of the actual intent of the authors of the legislation. I conclude without hesitation that I must answer that question in the affirmative.

Aiding Disadvantaged Groups

Bakke and *Weber* have been decided and are now an important part of the fabric of our law. This consideration is sufficiently compelling for me to adhere to the basic construction of this legislation that the Court adopted in *Bakke* and in *Weber.* There is an undoubted public interest in "stability and orderly development of the law."

The logic of antidiscrimination legislation requires that judicial constructions of Title VII leave "breathing room" for employer initiatives to benefit members of minority groups. If Title VII had never been enacted, a private employer would be free to hire members of minority groups for any reason that might seem sensible from a business or a social point of view. The Court's opinion in *Weber* reflects the same approach; the opinion relied heavily on legislative history indicating that Congress intended that traditional management prerogatives be left undisturbed to the greatest extent possible. As we observed Last Term, "'[i]t would be ironic indeed if a law triggered by a Nation's concern over centuries of racial injustice and intended to improve the lot of those who had "been excluded from the American dream for so long" constituted the first legislative prohibition of all voluntary, private, race-conscious efforts to abolish traditional patterns of racial segregation and hierarchy.'" *Firefighters* v. *Cleveland,* (1986). In *Firefighters,* we again acknowledged Congress' concern in Title VII to avoid "undue federal interference with managerial discretion."

"Public and private employers might choose to implement affirmative action for many reasons other than to purge their own past sins of discrimination."

As construed in *Weber* and in *Firefighters,* the statute does not absolutely prohibit preferential hiring in favor of minorities; it was merely intended to protect historically disadvantaged groups *against* discrimination and not to hamper managerial efforts to benefit members of disadvantaged groups that are consistent with that paramount purpose. The preference granted by respondent in this case does not violate the statute as so construed; the record amply supports the conclusion that the challenged employment decision served the legitimate purpose of creating diversity in a category of employment that had been almost an exclusive province of males in the past. Respondent's voluntary decision is surely not prohibited by Title VII as construed in *Weber.*

Looking Forward

Whether a voluntary decision of the kind made by respondent would ever be prohibited by Title VII is a question we need not answer until it is squarely presented. Given the interpretation of the statute the Court adopted in *Weber,* I see no reason why the employer has any duty, prior to granting a preference to a qualified minority employee, to

determine whether his past conduct might constitute an arguable violation of Title VII. Indeed, in some instances the employer may find it more helpful to focus on the future. Instead of retroactively scrutinizing his own or society's possible exclusions of minorities in the past to determine the outer limits of a valid affirmative-action program—or indeed, any particular affirmative-action decision—in many cases the employer will find it more appropriate to consider other legitimate reasons to give preferences to members of under-represented groups. Statutes enacted for the benefit of minority groups should not block these forward-looking considerations.

> Public and private employers might choose to implement affirmative action for many reasons other than to purge their own past sins of discrimination. The Jackson school board, for example, said it had done so in part to improve the quality of education in Jackson—whether by improving black students' performance or by dispelling for black and white students alike any idea that white supremacy governs our social institutions. Other employers might advance different forward-looking reasons for affirmative action: improving their services to black constituencies, averting racial tension over the allocation of jobs in a community, or increasing the diversity of a work force, to name but a few examples. Or they might adopt affirmative action simply to eliminate from their operations all de facto embodiment of a system of racial caste. All of these reasons aspire to a racially integrated future, but none reduces to 'racial balancing for its own sake.' Sullivan, "The Supreme Court—Comment, Sins of Discrimination: Last Term's Affirmative Action Cases," 100 *Harvard Law Review* 78, 96 (1986).

The Court today does not foreclose other voluntary decisions based in part on a qualified employee's membership in a disadvantaged group. Accordingly, I concur.

John Paul Stevens is a member of the United States Supreme Court.

"[The Court] effectively replace[d] the goal of a discrimination-free society with the quite incompatible goal of proportionate representation by race and by sex."

viewpoint **117**

The Supreme Court Made the Wrong Decision in *Johnson*

Antonin Scalia

Editor's note: The following viewpoint is the dissenting opinion of Justice Antonin Scalia on the Supreme Court's March 25, 1987 ruling in Paul E. Johnson v. The Transportation Agency of Santa Clara County, *California.*

Title VII of the Civil Rights Act of 1964 declares:

> It shall be an unlawful employment practice for an employer—
> "(1) to fail or refuse to hire or to discharge any individual, or otherwise to discriminate against any individual with respect to his compensation, terms, conditions, or privileges of employment, because of such individual's race, color, religion, sex, or national origin; or
> "(2) to limit, segregate, or classify his employees or applicants for employment in any way which would deprive or tend to deprive any individual of employment opportunities or otherwise adversely affect his status as an employee, because of such individual's race, color, religion, sex, or national origin."

The Court today completes the process of converting this from a guarantee that race or sex will *not* be the basis for employment determinations, to a guarantee that it often *will*. Ever so subtly, without even alluding to the last obstacles preserved by earlier opinions that we now push out of our path, we effectively replace the goal of a discrimination-free society with the quite incompatible goal of proportionate representation by race and by sex in the workplace. . . .

No Past Discrimination

On October 16, 1979, the County of Santa Clara adopted an Affirmative Action Program (County plan) which sought the "attainment of a County work force whose composition . . . includes women, disabled persons and ethnic minorities in a ratio in

all job categories that reflects their distribution in the Santa Clara County area work force." In order to comply with the County plan and various requirements imposed by federal and state agencies, the Transportation Agency adopted, effective December 18, 1978, the Equal Employment Opportunity Affirmative Action Plan at issue here. Its stated long-range goal was the same as the County plan's: "to attain a work force whose composition in all job levels and major job classifications approximates the distribution of women, minority and handicapped persons in the Santa Clara County work force." The plan called for the establishment of a procedure by which Division Directors would review the ethnic and sexual composition of their work forces whenever they sought to fill a vacancy, which procedure was expected to include "a requirement that Division Directors indicate why they did *not* select minorities, women and handicapped persons if such persons were on the list of eligibles considered and if the Division had an underrepresentation of such persons in the job classification being filled." (Emphasis in original.)

Several salient features of the plan should be noted. Most importantly, the plan's purpose was assuredly not to remedy prior sex discrimination by the Agency. It could not have been, because there was no prior sex discrimination to remedy. The majority, in cataloguing the Agency's alleged misdeeds, neglects to mention the District Court's finding that the Agency "has not discriminated in the past, and does not discriminate in the present against women in regard to employment opportunities in general and promotions in particular." This finding was not disturbed by the Ninth Circuit.

Not only was the plan not directed at the results of past sex discrimination by the Agency, but its objective was not to achieve the state of affairs that

Antonin Scalia, dissenting opinion of the Supreme Court in the case of Paul E. Johnson, petitioner v. Transportation Agency, Santa Clara County, California, March 25, 1987.

america's economy/71

this Court has dubiously assumed would result from an absence of discrimination—an overall work force "more or less representative of the racial and ethnic composition of the population in the community." *Teamsters* v. *United States*, (1977). Rather, the oft-stated goal was to mirror the racial and sexual composition of the entire county labor force, not merely in the Agency work force as a whole, but in each and every individual job category at the Agency. In a discrimination-free world, it would obviously be a statistical oddity for every job category to match the racial and sexual composition of even that portion of the county work force *qualified* for that job; it would be utterly miraculous for each of them to match, as the plan expected, the composition of the *entire* work force. Quite obviously, the plan did not seek to replicate what a lack of discrimination would produce, but rather imposed racial and sexual tailoring that would, in defiance of normal expectations and laws of probability, give each protected racial and sexual group a governmentally determined "proper" proportion of each job category....

Forcing Affirmative Action

The one message that the plan unmistakably communicated was that concrete results were expected, and supervisory personnel would be evaluated on the basis of the affirmative-action numbers they produced. The plan's implementation was expected to "result in a statistically measurable yearly improvement in the hiring, training and promotion of minorities, women and handicapped persons in the major job classifications utilized by the Agency where these groups are underrepresented." Its Preface declared that "[t]he degree to which each Agency Division *attains the Plan's objectives* will provide a direct measure of that Division Director's personal commitment to the EEO Policy," and the plan itself repeated that "[t]he degree to which each Division *attains the Agency Affirmative Action employment goals* will provide a measure of that Director's commitment and effectiveness in carrying out the Division's EEO Affirmative Action requirements." As noted earlier, supervisors were reminded of the need to give attention to affirmative action in every employment decision, and to explain their reasons for *failing* to hire women and minorities whenever there was an opportunity to do so.

The petitioner in the present case, Paul E. Johnson, had been an employee of the Agency since 1967, coming there from a private company where he had been a road dispatcher for seventeen years. He had first applied for the position of Road Dispatcher at the Agency in 1974, coming in second. Several years later, after a reorganization resulted in a downgrading of his Road Yard Clerk II position, in which Johnson "could see no future," he requested

and received a voluntary demotion from Road Yard Clerk II to Road Maintenance Worker, to increase his experience and thus improve his chances for future promotion. When the Road Dispatcher job next became vacant, in 1979, he was the leading candidate—and indeed was assigned to work out of class full-time in the vacancy, from September of 1979 until June of 1980. There is no question why he did not get the job....

The Favored MQs

The majority emphasizes, as though it is meaningful, that "*No* persons are automatically excluded from consideration; *all* are able to have their qualifications weighed against those of other applicants." One is reminded of the exchange from Shakespeare's King Henry the Fourth, Part I: "*Glendower:* I can call Spirits from the vasty Deep. *Hotspur:* Why, so can I, or so can any man. But will they come when you do call for them?" Act III, Scene I, lines 53-55. Johnson was indeed entitled to have his qualifications weighed against those of other applicants—but more to the point, he was virtually assured that, after the weighing, if there was any minimally qualified applicant from one of the favored groups, he would be rejected.

> "Johnson was virtually assured that . . . if there was any minimally qualified applicant from one of the favored groups, he would be rejected."

Similarly hollow is the Court's assurance that we would strike this plan down if it "failed to take distinctions in qualifications into account," because that "would dictate mere blind hiring by the numbers." For what the Court means by "taking distinctions in qualifications into account" consists of no more than eliminating from the applicant pool those who are not even *minimally qualified* for the job. Once that has been done, once the promoting officer assures himself that all the candidates before him are "M.Q.s" (minimally qualifieds), he can then ignore, as the Agency Director did here, how much better than minimally qualified some of the candidates may be, and can proceed to appoint from the pool solely on the basis of race or sex, until the affirmative action "goals" have been reached. The requirement that the employer "take distinctions in qualifications into account" thus turns out to be an assurance, not that candidates' comparative merits will always be considered, but only that none of the successful candidates selected over the others solely on the basis of their race or sex will be utterly unqualified. That may be of great comfort to those concerned with American productivity; and it is undoubtedly effective in reducing the effect of affirmative-action discrimination upon those in the upper strata of society, who (unlike road maintenance workers, for example) compete for employment in professional and semiprofessional fields where, for many reasons, including most notably the effects of past discrimination, the numbers of "M.Q." applicants from the favored groups are substantially less. But I fail to see how it has any relevance to whether selecting among final candidates solely on the basis of race or sex is permissible under Title VII, which prohibits discrimination on the basis of race or sex. . . .

The Losers

It is unlikely that today's result will be displeasing to politically elected officials, to whom it provides the means of quickly accommodating the demands of organized groups to achieve concrete, numerical improvement in the economic status of particular constituencies. Nor will it displease the world of corporate and governmental employers (many of whom have filed briefs as *amici* in the present case, all on the side of Santa Clara) for whom the cost of hiring less qualified workers is often substantially less—and infinitely more predictable—than the cost of litigating Title VII cases and of seeking to convince federal agencies by nonnumerical means that no discrimination exists. In fact, the only losers in the process are the Johnsons of the country, for whom Title VII has been not merely repealed but actually inverted. The irony is that these individuals—predominantly unknown, unaffluent, unorganized—suffer this injustice at the hands of a Court fond of thinking itself the champion of the politically impotent. I dissent.

Antonin Scalia is a member of the United States Supreme Court.

"The prospects for American agriculture are not good for the next few years, and [are] uncertain after that."

The Farm Crisis Is Real

Christopher Larson

President Reagan signed a farm bill last December [1985] that was a tribute to the art of compromise— everyone could find something in it to be unhappy about. Farmers saddled with high debts and weak markets complained that the bill would lower the prices for their crops. The bill's cost—estimated at $169 billion over its five-year lifetime, including $85 billion in programs to help farmers—gave little solace to those who wanted to cut the federal deficit. And while the legislation incorporated new provisions to safeguard farmland, environmentalists were discontented with the amount of time that will elapse before some of these measures are to take effect.

That the bill did not satisfy anyone's wish list is partly a reflection of the give and take of politics. It is also, however, a measure of the difficulties confronting American agriculture. Farm state legislators make up a powerful bloc in Washington. If times were better, and if the help farmers needed was not as great, perhaps they would have obtained a bill that gave them pretty much what they wanted. But with the agricultural sector as depressed as it is, and the present political climate as budget-conscious as it is, one can hardly be surprised that the farmers' demands were not wholly met—especially given the Reagan administration's ideological commitment to the free market.

The background to the legislative tale was what has become known as the "farm crisis." With as many as one-third of the country's commercial farmers experiencing financial difficulties, public attention has naturally focused on agriculture's immediate problems. After all, if you're worried about meeting payment on a note that's due next month, speculation about where you'll be in 10 or

20 years is a luxury.

And yet, the future of agriculture is a matter of vital public interest. Perhaps surprisingly, given the way present concerns tend to take priority in many legislators' minds, the debate in Congress actually turned, to a great extent, upon conflicting visions of this future. On one side were the administration and others who foresee a high-tech, market-based agriculture. On the other were those who pleaded the values of an endangered rural way of life. The final legislation was a compromise, but establishing a cash figure acceptable to both sides does not end the disparity between the two points of view.

Problems of a Strong Dollar

The business of agriculture in America is both big and complex. The industry as a whole—from farming to the retailing of farm products—accounts for a fifth of our gross national product, making it the largest single sector of the economy. Agriculture has traditionally been a major source of exports for the United States; to supply just our own food needs would require only two-thirds of our current agricultural base. As with other American export industries, farmers' present difficulties stem in part from the strong dollar. When a foreign country wishes to buy grain, and it can choose whether to buy from a country that accepts, say, Brazilian cruzeiros, which are cheap, or American dollars, which aren't, American farmers will inevitably lose sales.

In a textbook free market economy, the situation would resolve itself simply: American farmers would just slash prices until they could sell their output. Those who could not manage to turn a profit in this fashion would go out of business. The Reagan camp seemed to favor this logic-of-the-market approach when the debate over the farm bill started. Political realities intervened, and the bill ultimately continued government programs that regulate the market. The

Christopher Larson, "The Problems of Plenty" *Northwest Orient*, March 1986. Reprinted courtesy *Northwest Orient* magazine carried aboard Northwest Orient airlines. © 1986. East/West Network, Inc. publisher.

administration, however, won a philosophical commitment to moving in the direction of the market.

A strong dollar is not the only source of woe. Farmers are also paying the price now for an expansionary period in the 1970s during which they went heavily into debt to buy land and equipment. The vision then was that America would become the breadbasket of the world. Export demand would buoy up prices, and farmers could plant from fencerow to fencerow. When the bubble burst, farmers were holding mortages at high interest rates while their incomes were declining. In many areas, land values plummeted. According to Robert Jolly, an economist at Iowa State University, the average price of an acre of Iowa farmland rose from $450 in the early 1970s to $2,150 a decade later, but has since fallen back to $950.

In the Danger Zone

The ratio of a farm's debts to its assets—of which the land itself is the prime constituent—is cited by a United States Department of Agriculture study as a key indicator of the farm's financial health. A debt-asset ratio of 40 percent or more indicates possible financial trouble. Almost a third of the commercial farms in the U.S. are in this danger zone. Some of these farms generate sufficient cash flow to avoid serious difficulty, but about 20 percent of the country's commercial farms have the combination of "high debt load" and inadequate income that the department calls "financial stress."

"Almost a third of the commercial farms in the U.S. are in this danger zone."

(How many farms are there in the U.S.? The figures vary, according to who's counting and what criteria are used. Estimates range from 1.7 million to 2.4 million, the lesser figure excluding a number of farms that produce only a modest amount of goods for sale. These are often operations run by "gentlemen farmers" who derive most of their income from other sources. If a commercial farm is defined as one with $40,000 or more in annual sales—the most common definition—then there are around 650,000 of them in the United States, accounting for 90 percent of all farm sales.)

Debt and a strong dollar would not weigh so heavily if grain and other commodities were in short supply on world markets. However, they are not—at least not in those parts of the world that can afford to buy them. Overproduction and surpluses are the underlying causes of farmers' financial troubles, as they have been for decades. Every farmer, of course, wants a good harvest. But when every farmer gets

one, prices fall. In looking to the future, one can predict that the dollar will eventually weaken and debt will eventually be reduced, partly through government help and partly because the farmers hit hardest will be forced out of business. But if American farmers keep on producing more than the world is willing or able to buy, their financial prospects will remain dim.

The situation is an affront to our sense of rightness: it seems absurd to speak of overproduction when hundreds of millions of people around the world are malnourished. Unfortunately, the countries that most need food can't buy it. We can and do give food as foreign aid, cutting our surpluses while simultaneously serving humanitarian and foreign policy ends. But giving food away is not really a solution to the problem of getting a decent price for it. Nor is the aid always trouble-free for the recipient nations, because it may, in effect, compete with the products of struggling local farmers.

Limiting Production

One answer to a weak market is to limit production. The American government seeks to do this by its well-known and much-maligned policy of persuading farmers to let land lay fallow. Keeping a certain percentage of acres out of production is a condition for loans and participation in target price programs. If the government still believes that too much land will be planted, it offers to pay farmers to keep more acres idle. These payments are a drain on the budget, but the reasoning is that if production is kept down, the market will improve, and therefore target price guarantees won't cost so much.

It's a fine idea in theory, but the system does not always work. Farmers enroll in the program, and then use fertilizers and everything else at their command to maximize the output of the acres they have planted. This makes perfect economic sense for each farmer individually, but it doesn't alleviate surpluses. If we returned to the agricultural technology of the 1940s, our capacity would balance our domestic needs, but why would we choose to do that?

Patrick M. O'Brien, the deputy associate administrator for outlook and situation of the Department of Agriculture's Economic Research Service, does not see the near future in an optimistic light. We can "pray that the exchange rate goes down," he says; beyond that, we have to "hope for the best and stick it out for a few years." Recent grain deficits, especially during the 1970s, caused large amounts of new acreage to be brought into production around the world; even though the present grain surpluses have made further expansion senseless, it will be some time before consumption grows enough to soak up the existing oversupply.

Consumption, of course, will grow with rising populations and standards of living. But there is no question that some people in the United States will be forced out of farming before a turnaround occurs. And farmers' groups are worried about the longer-term prospects as well. Recent advances in the People's Republic of China and India indicate a realization around the world that a strong agricultural sector is of key importance. Our country welcomes this trend, but a decreased reliance on American exports will not help our own situation. . . .

Uncertain Prospects

Barring a string of bad harvests in the countries we compete with, the prospects for American agriculture are not good for the next few years, and uncertain after that. A small percentage of farmers will fail; most will make do, some with the assistance of government programs and some without it. Farmers tend to view themselves more as producers than as marketers, and as producers they can claim exceptional success. But they have not enjoyed equal success in the marketplace, and consequently many cannot hope for much more than to scrape by and hope for better times.

"There is no question that some people in the United States will be forced out of farming before a turnaround occurs."

Such is not the case in the countries of the European Economic Community, which shelters its farmers under an expensive system of price supports called the Common Agricultural Policy. CAP accounts for the lion's share of the EEC's budget, and the policy has drawn attacks from many proponents of free trade as a protectionist system that subsidizes inefficient producers. But Robert Frederick, the legislative director for the National Grange, a powerful lobbying organization, offers a different assessment. The common market countries, he says, decided to preserve their threatened agricultural sector as a question of social policy. The decision was taken, he says, in light of their awareness that the smokestack industries that formerly provided a haven to those workers displaced from farming were themselves in trouble.

The point of these observations about Europe is that America, in Frederick's view, is on the point of facing a similar decision—whether, as a matter of national policy, to take the steps necessary to ensure the well-being of the country's farmers. Lacking such a decision, he argues, "a segment of society called rural America could soon be gone."

In essence, Frederick and other lobbyists are saying that farmers cannot rely on the market. Congress listens to such appeals with sympathy—witness the billions of dollars voted for farm programs. But it is extremely hard, for a number of reasons, to imagine our government making an explicit commitment on the order of the EEC's.

For one thing, despite current difficulties and uncertain prospects, farmers here are in general more efficient than their European counterparts: for Americans, surviving the rigors of the market is a less impossible goal. Also, the desire to preserve rural communities must be balanced by the knowledge that this country's history is that of people leaving the farm: after the proportion of farmers has dropped steadily over the decades, from an estimated 90 percent during the Revolutionary War era to 3 percent today, a further fall to 2.5 percent does not seem disastrous. Finally, there is our political commitment to a market economy. It is one thing for Congress to vote aid at a particular time in response to depressed conditions. It is another to repudiate the market permanently.

Settling for Compromise

So Congress compromises. Farmers get enough help so that most of them can survive, but the ideal and claims of a market-based economy are reaffirmed. There is a tendency for people in the field to believe that the harsh imperatives of the market will promote consolidation and agribusiness—the corporate ownership of large farms. But it is not clear that the facts support this notion. Much of American agriculture has already achieved the size that is feasible to its continued operation. What the present austere climate does probably mean is that American agriculture will have to become leaner and even more efficient. Family farms have been accomplishing this for generations, but it will continue to be—excuse the metaphor—a hard row to hoe.

Christopher Larson writes frequently on American social issues.

"The debate in Congress and in the media distorted and oversimplified the situation on the farm."

viewpoint **119**

The Farm Crisis Is a Myth

James L. Gattuso

Debates about federal agricultural policy often are long on emotion and rhetoric and short on facts. At no time was this more apparent than during congressional consideration of the Food Security Act of 1985, which set a five-year program for federal farm policy. To be sure, there are problems in U.S. agriculture, but the debate in Congress and in the media distorted and oversimplified the situation on the farm. One of the more ludicrous moments in the debate was the appearance before a congressional committee by a trio of Hollywood "farm movie" actresses to give their view of the agricultural situation. The image makers had become the experts.

Today, barely fifteen months since passage of the Food Security Act, the legislation is generally considered a failure. Despite the expenditure of a record $25.8 billion in Fiscal Year 1986 and an expected $25.2 billion in Fiscal Year 1987, the condition of American agriculture has not changed significantly. Congress thus is gearing up for a new farm bill. The proposals offered by lawmakers range from reducing Washington's control over farmers to imposing mandatory limits, set by Washington, on what each American farmer can grow.

Five Myths

As policy makers begin this review process, they should separate fact from fiction, and Hollywood from reality. They should discard the myths that have befogged farm policy debates in the past, including:

1) *Farmers are generally poor.* The fact: The average net worth of U.S. farms is over a quarter of a million dollars, and the average income of farm operators exceeds $30,000, much higher than that of most Americans.

2) *Most farmers are in deep debt trouble.* The fact:

While debt problems have increased, a majority of farmers are still relatively unburdened by debt. Almost 80 percent have debt-to-asset ratios of under 40 percent, with an average of about 10 percent each.

3) *Farmers are leaving the land at unprecedented rates.* The fact: The rate of decrease in the number of farms and in farm population has been much lower in recent years than in the 1950s and 1960s.

4) *The family farm is disappearing.* The fact: Only about 7,000 of the nation's farms, and one and one-half percent of the land, is owned by corporations. The "family farm" is not disappearing, although it is changing.

5) *Federal subsidies go to farmers in need.* The fact: The majority of these subsidies go to large, well-off farmers, and are not effectively directed to those who need them most.

Farmers Are Generally Poor

Most U.S. farmers are not poor, despite what Hollywood and television portray. In fact, in terms of assets, the average farmer is doing quite well. According to the U.S. Department of Agriculture (USDA), the average U.S. farm (including land, equipment, and inventory) has a net worth of $251,963. The largest farms—those with annual sales of half a million dollars or more—have an average net worth of $1,685,350. But even the smallest farms have significant net worths. The lowest income category of farms—those with sales of less than $10,000 per year—have an average net worth of about $135,000. Farms with sales of $100,000 to $250,000, mostly owned by full-time "family" farmers, have a net worth of over $350,000.

In terms of net worth, farmers are far wealthier than the average American. Some 61 percent of farm households have a net worth of over $100,000. Barely 21 percent of all Americans have a net worth that high. Over 11 percent of farm households have

James L. Gattuso, "Five Myths About the State of the American Farmer," The Heritage Foundation *Backgrounder*, March 18, 1987. Reprinted with permission.

over $500,000 in net worth, compared with less than 2 percent of all Americans.

The average farmer can hardly be considered poor in terms of annual income. . . . The net cash income of U.S. farm operators was $13,479 in 1985. The largest farm operators averaged $237,597 in net cash income from farming, while the smallest farmers, the so-called "hobby" farmers, where the owners do not depend on the farm for their income, operated at an average loss of $3,058. The income of the middle-sized farmers ranged from just under $11,000 to over $32,000.

Farm income alone, however, does not tell the full story of the income available to farmers. Most farmers derive a significant amount of their income from off-farm jobs, sometimes working 100 or 200 days a year off the farm. On average, each farm operator received $22,757 in such off-farm income in 1985, and farmers in the $40,000-$100,000 sales class typically received over $19,000 in off-farm income.

"Most U.S. farmers are not poor, despite what Hollywood and television portray."

Thus the average farmer received over $36,000 in total income in 1985. This is more than $8,000 higher than the $27,765 median annual income for all American families in 1985. Even middle-sized farmers in the $100,000-$250,000 sales class did much better than the U.S. median, with approximately $44,000 in income. Those in the lower middle range, however, with $40,000-$100,000 in sales, had about $24,000 in total income.

These are average figures, of course, and within each category of farm there are many farmers making less than the average or even suffering large losses. As in the case of any other group of American businessmen and women, some farmers are poor, many are in the middle, and many are wealthy.

Farmers Are in Deep Debt Trouble

The debt burden on farmers has increased substantially over the last several years. According to the Congressional Research Service, farmers' debt-to-asset ratio (the amount they owe compared with their assets) increased from 18.8 percent in 1981 to an estimated 25 percent in 1986. Yet total farm debt actually decreased by about 1 percent during this time. The increase in the ratio has been caused not by an increase in debt, but by a 25 percent decrease in farm assets, caused mainly by falling land values. Despite the recent increase, the debt levels in agriculture are much lower than in many other industries. Example: The debt-asset ratio for

manufacturing corporations exceeds 50 percent.

The debt ratio situation, moreover, has not affected all farmers uniformly. According to a recent General Accounting Office report, 78.7 percent of farms had debt-to-asset ratios of 40 percent or less in 1985. On average, the debt carried by these farmers was only about 10 percent of their assets.

Only a small percentage of farms are in severe debt trouble. Less than 5 percent of American farms, for instance, had debt-to-asset ratios in 1985 between 70 percent and 100 percent, while a mere 4 percent were technically insolvent with debt ratios of over 100 percent. Admittedly, the number of such farms is increasing—it was 3 percent in 1984—and the financial condition of these farms cannot be taken lightly. Yet they constitute a very small fraction of farms.

Farmers Are Leaving the Land

The farm population is shrinking. From 1981 to 1986 the number of farms decreased by 220,000, and the total farm population decreased by 624,000. However, this decrease is nothing new. It conforms to a long-term trend in this and other countries. The American farm population has been steadily shrinking through most of this century and has been decreasing as a percent of the total U.S. population ever since records were first kept. In 1900, for example, over 40 percent of Americans lived on farms. This figure decreased to about 15 percent by 1960, and stands at 2.2 percent today.

In fact, the rate at which farmers have been leaving agriculture in the last few years has been quite low compared with earlier periods. The great exodus from farming reached its peak about 30 years ago. In 1950, there were about 5.6 million farms in America. By 1955, this number had decreased to about 4.7 million, or a drop of over 17 percent in just five years. And by 1975, there were about 2.5 million farms, a decrease of over 50 percent in 25 years. Between 1950 and 1970, the number of Americans living on farms decreased by almost 58 percent, from about 23 million to just over 9.7 million.

During the 1970s, this exodus almost stopped entirely, as agriculture enjoyed nearly a decade of prosperity. From 1975 to 1980, the number of farms decreased by just 3.5 percent. More striking, the number of Americans employed in agriculture stayed about even. Indeed, there were actually 7,000 more Americans employed in agriculture in 1982 than there were in 1971.

The exodus from farming has resumed in the 1980s, but at a much lower rate. From 1980 to 1985, the number of U.S. farms decreased only 6.1 percent, less than half the rate seen in the 1950s and 1960s. Overall, the percentage decrease in the number of farms between 1975 and 1985 was the smallest the nation had seen in any decade since the

1930s. In absolute terms, the difference is even more striking. During the 1950s, the number of farms decreased by over one and a half million. From 1975 to 1985, the decrease was less than 250,000—one-sixth the decrease in the 1950s. In fact, almost as many farms closed in 1952 alone as were lost during that entire period.

Similarly, the farm population dropped only 9.1 percent between 1981 and 1985, a fraction of the declines experienced earlier. The Census Bureau reported in February that it found 129,000 fewer people living on farms in 1986, a change that it said was "not a statistically significant decline" compared with 1985. While almost seven and a half million Americans left the land during the 1950s, barely one-tenth that number have left since 1981.

The Family Farm Is Disappearing

According to the most recent Census of Agriculture, the vast majority of American farms are still operated by families or individuals. As of 1982, 86.9 percent of American farms were owned by families or individuals, and they farmed over 75 percent of all U.S. cropland. Another 10 percent of farms, representing about 16 percent of cropland, were owned by partnerships. Only 2.7 percent of farms and 13.6 percent of farmland were owned by corporations. The vast majority of these corporations, moreover, actually were family-owned. Only about 7,000 farms, holding about 1.5 percent of farmland, were owned by nonfamily corporations.

Of course, most of the farms that are family-owned do not really fit in the category of "family farm." That term has come to mean much more than technical ownership by a family. It connotes a way of life, where the farm is big enough to support a family, but not so big that the family hires employees to operate the farm.

"Only a small percentage of farms are in severe debt trouble."

The majority of U.S. farms are too small to be considered family farms in this sense. About 70 percent of farms bring in $40,000 or less in gross sales each year. These farms rarely are a major source of income for their operators. In 1985, in fact, they averaged a $1,635 loss each. But these farms usually are not intended to support families. They are for the most part operated as hobbies or as sources of extra income for Americans who work in the city. For instance, such farmers may work full-time in a nearby town in another job, but work their farm on weekends for extra cash or relaxation.

At the other end of the spectrum are large farms, with gross sales of $250,000 or more. They are small

in number, about 93,000, or 4.1 percent of all farms. Nevertheless, these farms are responsible for close to half the gross farm income each year.

In the middle are farms with gross sales of roughly $40,000 to $250,000. It is in this group that most farms considered family farms can be found. This category includes about a fourth of all farms and produces about 40 percent of gross income.

And this class of farms has been struggling the most in recent years. Yet they are not "disappearing." In fact, the share of total sales produced by large and small farms has remained remarkably constant over the last 25 years. The largest 1 percent of farms accounted for roughly 30 percent of production in 1960 and account for about the same proportion today. At the other end of the scale, one-half of U.S. farms accounted for only 3 percent of production in 1960, the same as their share today.

While family-type farms are not disappearing, they have been changing vastly over the years. They are very different from the idealized Norman Rockwell farms pictured in popular literature, box-office movie hits, and congressional rhetoric. They are not being taken over by large, monolithic corporations, they are becoming more businesslike themselves. . . .

Needy Farmers Get Subsidies

Federal farm programs are usually defended as an essential means of helping struggling farmers, who otherwise would not be able to make it on their own. The truth is, only a small portion of the federal grants, subsidies, loans, and other funds ever reaches struggling family farmers. Federal funding for farmers is concentrated in certain sectors of U.S. agriculture. Crops such as wheat, corn, and cotton, receive substantial subsidies. But other crops, representing about half of U.S. agricultural production, including vegetables, fruit, cattle, hogs, and poultry, operate very successfully without direct subsidies.

In the case of those crops that do operate with subsidies, they go disproportionately to the largest farms. Of the $7.7 billion in direct federal payments made to farmers in 1985, 13.3 percent went to the 1.3 percent that were the largest U.S. farms—those with annual sales of $500,000 or more. Almost a third of all direct payments were made to farms with sales of $250,000 or more, although they constitute only 4.1 percent of U.S. farms. And over two-thirds of government payments went to farms with over $100,000 in sales, constituting less than 14 percent of all farms. This maldistribution results in bonanzas for many large farmers. One company in California's San Joaquin Valley, for instance, collected over $20 million in benefits in 1986. Another company in Texas, partly owned by the crown prince of Liechtenstein, received $2.2 million in subsidies from the taxpayers last year.

Those farmers experiencing financial difficulties, meanwhile, receive only a small share of federal funds. Only about 24 percent went to farmers operating in the red. Of these, only about two-thirds had debt-to-asset ratios of 40 percent or more. The USDA usually considers a farmer to be "financially stressed" if he or she has a debt-to-asset ratio of 40 percent or more and has a negative cash flow. Thus, under this definition, only about 16 percent of the federal money distributed in 1985 actually went to farmers in financial stress. Conversely, not all of the farms defined as financially stressed received assistance. According to the same study, only half of the farms in financial trouble received any payments at all.

"Debates on farm issues . . . too often tend to be based on misconceptions about the current state of the American farmer."

The reason for the gross maldistribution of benefits in the farm programs is simple. Subsidies are calculated not according to need, but according to the annual production of each farm. Thus, a large, financially secure farm can be eligible for a big subsidy payment while a struggling farmer with a small crop receives less help.

Conclusion

Congress soon will be considering a wide range of legislation intended to help the American farmer. Such a review is long overdue. The current farm programs cost over $25 billion last year and may be doing farmers more harm than good. Nevertheless, debates on farm issues in Congress and the media too often tend to be based on misconceptions about the current state of the American farmer.

In fashioning remedies for the acute problems of some farmers, policy makers must remember that farmers as a group are not generally poor. Some farmers are in deep financial trouble, but the vast majority are not. The decline in the number of farmers is part of a very long-term trend, but the family farm is not disappearing. And farm subsidies, however well-intentioned, are not going primarily to farmers who are in need. Carefully directed approaches, based on fact, are needed, not billions of federal dollars, based on fiction.

James L. Gattuso is a policy analyst at The Heritage Foundation in Washington, DC.

"For the health of our rural economy and the restoration of America's family farm tradition, . . . agricultural policy must be reversed."

viewpoint **120**

Government Should Help Save the Family Farm

Kevin Ristau

Agriculture supports over 21 percent of the nation's workforce, and is the single largest consumer of our own industrial products. Farm products themselves make up almost 70 percent of our annual raw materials production, and constitute renewable wealth—unlike oil, coal or other minerals.

But this enormous industry has been subjected to more than 30 years of national government policies designed intentionally to push out a large percentage of family farmers with prices rigged below the cost of production—"prices at the choking point," as one important policy-planning document of the 1960s approvingly put it.

A Tragic Social Problem

The current farm crisis, especially as it entails forced liquidations, is actually a culmination of policies promoted and followed in the United States since the end of World War II. While many of us see the loss of family farms as a tragic social problem, others consider it a necessary and natural "shaking out" and have made it a conscious objective.

In fact, the objective of removing more than half this country's family farms from existence has already been attained. The number of family workers in agriculture dropped from 18.1 million in 1946 to 2.2 million in 1983, according to the President's Council of Economic Advisers.

Our present predicament—the most serious rural crisis since the 1930s depression—raises the new and pressing question: "Who will own and control the enormous assets still left in the hands of America's farming community?" This wealth, which exceeds the total value of all U.S. manufacturing assets, represents the accumulated labor of many generations of farmers in this country. It's quite possible that over 50 percent of these assets will

pass into the hands of the nation's largest banks, insurance companies and corporations in the next five years.

The fundamental problem is a simple cost/price squeeze. While almost all farm expenses have increased in cost, prices paid to farmers for their products have remained low, with most crop prices currently at around 50 percent of parity (parity is a cost-of-living index for farmers that takes into account all production costs and computes a farmer's wages on a par with an urban worker with similar skills and responsibilities).

For example, corn prices are around $2.00 per bushel while parity price would be close to $4.00. Even the U.S. Department of Agriculture figures that the "cost of production" for corn (not including the cost of land or the farmer's labor) is around $3.00. The financial loss due to low crop prices is obviously staggering. The state of Iowa alone, for example, produces a billion bushels of corn each year and so Iowa farmers lose about a billion dollars on that corn.

When farmers are in serious trouble they can't fuel the rest of the economy. Farmers losing money don't buy many tractors or pick-up trucks, and they don't pay any taxes. What they did do, until recently, is borrow ever-increasing amounts of money from banks, insurance companies and the U.S. government just to stay alive. Between 1970 and 1984, total U.S. farm debt rose from around $20 billion to about $230 billion. During more than a decade of mostly low farm prices, this heavy borrowing contributed significantly to our rising interest rates.

With farmers and the businesses that supply them in trouble, tax revenues are sharply curtailed at the precise moment when demands made on government by the unemployed, by failing businesses and by collapsing banks are increasing. Although there has been a steady decline in the percentage of our population engaged in farming

Kevin Ristau, "U.S. Agriculture Policy Designed to Displace Family Farms," MPIRG *Statewatch*, January/February 1986. Reprinted with permission.

since colonial times, the present mass liquidations represent something other than technological or economic progress. Newspapers often describe the current crisis as "an inevitable result" of modernization or as a "tragedy of failed policies." But major policy documents from the past 40 years indicate that what we're actually witnessing is the result of successfully implemented policies designed to force farmers off the land.

Forcing Out the Family Farmer

Towards the end of World War II, the powerful and effective government-corporate-academic coalition constructed to guide the American war effort began to concern itself with impending peace. Dozens of policy planning committees issued long treatises on "the farm question" as a crucial component of post-war economic strategy. One of these, the Committee for Economic Development (CED) was formed in 1942 by the presidents of several large corporations and economists from the University of Chicago. Amongst the many reports, documents and proposals issued by this influential organization (academic and business members for three decades served as key U.S. agricultural policymakers) was "An Adaptive Program for Agriculture," released in 1962.

"When farmers are in serious trouble they can't fuel the rest of the economy."

CED shared the outlook of other elite planning councils after the war, most of which favored shifting approximately one-third of farm families— primarily the moderate-sized operations—out of agriculture. The strategy was to replace them with a small number of superfarms (large corporate-owned and a few family-managed operations), and several million "small farms" to be financed primarily by off-farm income or welfare. The large farms would identify and politically align with lenders and corporations investing in agribusiness; the small farmers' dependency on government and on the non-farm economy would weaken them politically and possibly diminish their traditional affiliation with progressive movements.

CED's 1962 report asserted that "the movement of people from agriculture has not been fast enough," and advocated "positive government action to facilitate and promote the movement of labor and capital where they will be most productive. . . ." Identifying the government's support of farm prices as a key impediment to labor flowing from agriculture, the CED program called for lower crop prices to "discourage further commitments of new productive resources to those crops unless it

appeared profitable at lower prices."

The report apparently was designed principally to serve the interests of the industrial, finance and trade corporations whose representatives made up CED membership. The results would be:

1) Increased return on corporate investment in agriculture;
2) Over two million farmers and families entering the urban labor pool;
3) Lower prices of agricultural products, which would both increase foreign trade and provide cheaper raw materials for domestic food and fiber processors.

CED's Below-Parity Prices

By 1974 the CED could claim success in having its general policies and aims followed and accomplished. Their evaluative follow-up report published in that year contained this summary:

> This statement examines the vast changes that have taken place in U.S. agriculture in the past decade. The reduction in the number of farms, the great increase in productivity, the industrialization of farming, and the urbanization of rural life have produced two readily identifiable agricultural sectors.
>
> One sector consists of large farms that, although numbering about 25 percent of all farms, produce 80 percent of all farm marketings. This group is engaged in the production of the major food and fiber crops such as grains, oilseeds and cotton. These products of commercial agriculture have been the focus of U.S. agriculture policy over the past 40 years and are now the major crops in world trade.
>
> The other 75 percent of U.S. farms, accounting for only 20 percent of the output, are operated largely by farmers who are increasingly dependent on the industrial and service sectors of the economy to provide supplemental or full-time employment. Where financial distress exists in this group, it is rooted mainly in general social and economic causes, not in farm prices. Assistance to these farmers should be extended not through special support programs but . . . through a national welfare assistance program.

The creation of a two-tiered system of agriculture—dominated by large, corporate or corporate-type farms, with the remaining majority farming part-time or on welfare—was the successful result of policies based on below-parity prices.

Farmers Protest Pricing Policies

Despite that these policies were advocated by some of the most powerful corporations in the United States and were bolstered by government and academic planners, protests and effective lobbying by farmers being liquidated slowed the process considerably. At the same time some farm leaders were pressured, cajoled or bribed to adopt "more reasonable" positions and to "abandon outdated concepts," like parity pricing.

Consumer groups and trade unions were consciously pitted against farmers, and the programs eventually forced on farmers were costly for taxpayers (unlike fair-price and production-management programs of the '30s and '40s, which made money for farmers *and* for the government).

One government response to late '60s and early '70s farm protest was the injection of more credit into the rural sector. When many farmers couldn't earn enough to repay their debts due to low prices, they were forced to mortgage more and more of their farm, which seemed manageable at 5 and 6 percent interest. But with current interest rates and today's drastically reduced value of land and equipment assets, many folks are being driven out of agriculture. Just as the planners and economists intended.

The shift in the structure of American agriculture since World War II has had secondary effects on farming practices in addition to the elimination of millions of farm families. Many characteristics of the industry can be traced directly to this shift:

- concentration of land ownership
- increasing farm debt
- decreasing soil conservation
- increased dependence on capital-intensive and fossil fuel-intensive methods
- inability of young, beginning or limited-resource farmers to stay in business.

The attempt to force farmers out of business by lowering prices paid them simply leads to overproduction. Just like any worker who gets his or her wages cut in half and still has bills to pay, farmers attempt to work twice as hard and produce twice as much. This can lead to abandonment of careful soil and water conservation practices and to the tilling of marginal, highly erodible land.

And our experience shows that as control over farmland has passed into the hands of large corporations and absentee investors, they have generally treated the irreplaceable natural resources with the same narrow, short-term profit orientation that has characterized their treatment of our capital resources such as factories and railroads. The earth is being used and abused as long as it can show a high enough profit or serve as a tax shelter for other profits. Once depleted, land is abandoned or covered over for "development" purposes. Ground water is being pumped and rivers diverted.

Enforced Low Crop Prices

Enforced low crop prices mean that corn which costs a highly efficient farmer more than $3.00 per bushel to produce is sold for just over $2.00, just as the best wheat farmers gets less than $3.10 per bushel when it costs them almost $5.00 to grow it. While this is often referred to as "cheap food policy," it clearly is actually a cheap *raw materials* policy.

The 1985 federal farm bill, for example, calls for forcing U.S. farm prices down even further, making it possible for grain exporting corporations to capture new markets overseas. Meanwhile, the corn for which the farmer receives around $2 per bushel is sold to U.S. consumers at over $200 per bushel in the form of processed breakfast cereals. And while farmers receive only 4 or 5 cents for the wheat in a loaf of bread, the consumer pays over a dollar.

President Reagan and his supporters in Congress believe that boosting demand for U.S. grain abroad will raise farm income over the long run. Since the United States sets world grain prices, the president assumes production in other countries can be discouraged by making prices so low that those countries' producers can't compete.

But since Europe and Japan protect their farmers economically, the United States is best able to "discourage" agricultural producers in the Third World, which is exactly what the administration proposes. By forcing U.S. farm prices below cost-of-production, with all the domestic consequences cited earlier, U.S.-based grain corporations can undersell local farmers in the domestic food markets of most Third World countries.

"Many folks are being driven out of agriculture. Just as the planners and economists intended."

Unable to earn a profit from farming, Third World farmers are driven off their farms and forced into overcrowded urban slums or shantytowns. The land they farmed may eventually erode or turn to desert. Or it may be absorbed into the large estate of an absentee landlord to produce cattle for export back to the United States. . . .

But today the end results are not simply the impoverishment of Third World farmers and the rural businesses and workers who depend on them for employment. The destruction of local farming and food production creates a dependency on food imports that must be paid for with precious hard currency. In many poor countries this amounts to a death sentence for millions of people. It forces governments to choose between importing food or importing medicines. . . .

To obtain fair prices and stop foreclosures, farmers and their organizations in the United States have developed a number of specific strategies and tactics, including advocacy of parity price legislation and foreclosure moratorium legislation. For the health of our rural economy and the restoration of America's family farm tradition, the recent trend in agricultural policy must be reversed.

Kevin Ristau is a staff member of the Minnesota League of Rural Voters.

Government Should Not Help Save the Family Farm

J. Bruce Bullock

Numerous economic and political factors are cited as having an adverse impact on American agriculture. High interest rates, the high value of the dollar, trade embargoes, unfair trade practices by our competitors, declining farmland values, widely fluctuating commodity prices, and commodity prices "below the cost of production" have all been named. The inability of a larger than usual number of farmers to meet debt obligations is offered as evidence that the combination of these factors and the U.S. government's "cheap food policy" is leading to the ruin of American agriculture. Surveys indicate that large numbers of farmers themselves perceive low commodity prices—and hence low farm income—as the problem, pointing to high interest rates and the high value of the dollar as important causes of it.

In fact, low commodity prices and low rates of return to management and capital in the agricultural sector are merely *symptoms*. Simply stated, the U.S. farm problem is one of an overinvestment of human and physical capital in the agricultural production sector. The symptoms of overinvestment in any sector of the economy are downward pressure on prices and lower rates of return to management and capital than in other sectors of the economy. High interest rates and the high value of the dollar compound the farm problem—but they are not its cause.

Withdraw Resources from Agriculture

The solution to the problem, difficult as it may seem, is to withdraw resources from agriculture until competitive rates of return are achieved. Many farmers and policymakers fail to accept the fact that agricultural production in the U.S. has evolved from a way of life to a high-technology, capital-intensive

J. Bruce Bullock, "What's Behind the Farm Problem." Reprinted from USA TODAY MAGAZINE, July 1986. Copyright 1986 by the Society for the Advancement of Education.

business. As a result, the economic signals to reduce investment in, and the output of, certain segments of the agricultural sector are viewed as a threat to a revered lifestyle, rather than as signals from market forces to alter the economic organization of the industry. Unfortunately, efforts to support commodity prices above market-clearing levels in order to maintain existing investments in agricultural production provide only partial and temporary symptomatic relief of the farm problem. Moreover, price-support programs seriously distort the clear signals for long-run adjustment being generated by the market.

It is often argued that, if the family farms are not saved, corporate farms will take over and charge the American consumer exorbitant prices for food. However, large corporations are simply not interested in high-risk investments that generate a three to five percent rate of return. Large corporations will be interested in agricultural investments only if they generate sustained rates of return in excess of other, less risky, and less complex investment opportunities. Raising the issue of corporate takeover of U.S. agriculture is a red herring.

The farm programs were developed about 50 years ago in response to prolonged chronic farm-income problems. At the time, 25% of the population lived on farms, and the income of the typical farm family was less than half that of an urban family. Most farms were about the same size, used similar technology, and employed similar management skills. Family labor and home-produced inputs accounted for a large part of the resources used by farmers. In this environment, price-support programs provided a relatively simple and effective method of improving farm income.

Farm programs throughout their history have reflected the view that farm-income problems are caused by a temporary imbalance in supply and demand. Thus, there has been a succession of short-run government programs designed to deal with the economic conditions in agriculture at the time the legislation was written, not an integrated farm policy that would facilitate long-term adjustments to the forces of change generated by new technology and market conditions.

Unsuccessful Government Programs

Today's basic agricultural programs are only slight modifications of the programs developed 50 years ago, and most of them have the dual objectives of price stability and income enhancement. In their simplest form, these programs have established minimum support prices through the use of crop loans, direct payments, and direct purchase of products, supplemented by various types of voluntary (subsidy-induced) or mandatory supply-reduction programs. Most supply-reduction programs have focused on reducing acreage planted.

"Many farmers and policymakers fail to accept the fact that agricultural production in the U.S. has evolved from a way of life to a high-technology, capital-intensive business."

In recent years, we have relied more heavily on voluntary supply-reduction programs. Voluntary programs have never been successful in reducing supplies over extended time periods, however, and they are never likely to be completely successful. Farmers quite understandably withdraw marginally productive land from production and expand their use of yield-increasing technology on the higher-quality land that remains in production. These programs also often provide strong incentives for the lowest-cost producers to expand output. Moreover, change in the agricultural sector has made it increasingly difficult and expensive to use voluntary supply-restriction programs to achieve income and price-support objectives.

Accepting the Change in Agriculture

There has been a phenomenal amount of change in U.S. agriculture in the past half-century, even with the existence of farm programs that have generally supported prices above market-clearing levels. The percentage of the U.S. population engaged in farming has decreased from about 25% in 1935 to less than 2.5% in 1985. The number of farms has fallen by more than 60% over that period.

In spite of the dramatic migration of people away from U.S. farms, American agricultural output has increased more rapidly than the demand for agricultural products. The result has been a continual recurrence of the symptoms of overinvestment in agriculture—low returns to management and capital. Existing farm programs were designed to treat the symptoms of the problem via price supports, rather than deal with the over-investment problem directly.

To their credit, farm programs have tended to soften the adjustment problems associated with moving human resources out of agriculture. The programs made it possible for most of the migration away from agriculture to occur through the retirement of farm operators, and their farmland was integrated into expanding farm operations. Younger members of farm families often moved on to more promising economic opportunities long before their parents retired. Thus, people moved out of agricultural production as new technology made it possible and desirable to substitute capital for labor in the U.S. agricultural sector. The amount of land used for agricultural production declined less than five percent since 1935, however, while output per acre more than doubled. Claims that we are running out of prime farmland are simply untrue.

Much of the current discussion about the changing structure of American agriculture has centered on the future of the family farm and on the effects of government farm policy. The continued injection of new capital-intensive production technology into the agricultural sector has eroded the usefulness of traditional farm programs as a moderator of change there. Changes in the nature of these programs are required if they are to reflect present economic realities. . . .

No Need To Support Farmers

There is an additional economic reality in the agricultural sector that should be considered. The per capita disposable income of farm operators has averaged 88% of nonfarm income over the past 10 years, in contrast to about 50% during the 1940s and 1950s and 60% in the 1960s. Given the favorable tax treatment of farmers, there is no longer any basis for arguing that farm incomes need to be supported relative to nonfarm incomes.

A major reason for the more narrow income gap between farm and nonfarm families is the increased access of farm families to nonfarm sources of income. Over 60% of the personal disposable income of farm operators comes from off-farm sources. On average, farm operators selling less than $20,000 per year obtained all their disposable income from off-farm sources. Only operators with over $100,000 in annual gross sales obtained more than half their disposable income from farm sources. Off-farm income accounted for over 99% of farm-family income for 72% of the "farms" in the U.S.

This leads to the conclusion that part of the

current policy problem is definitional. For public policy purposes, what should be considered a "farm"? The census definition of a farm is one with $1,000 gross sales of agricultural commodities. Numerous problems arise when the fact that farm prices are below the cost of production for 60% of U.S. farms is interpreted to mean that government should support agricultural income via some type of price-support program. The result is government programs that disrupt agricultural markets in order to support the income of farmers whose incomes do not need supporting. The programs' target group—small-scale, low-income farm operators—actually receives little, if any, direct benefits from the programs. In short, the current definition of a "farm" results in increasingly expensive and difficult-to-manage agricultural programs that are unjustifiable from a social-welfare point of view. The programs have the added drawback of stimulating further investment in the agricultural sector, rather than encouraging and facilitating disinvestment.

Redefining the Farm

From an economic perspective, overinvestment in the agricultural sector is concentrated in the 72% of the farms that produce only 13% of total agricultural products. These farms can not make a profit at current prices. Thus, a major portion of the farm problem could be eliminated by changing the definition of a "farm" to "an agricultural production unit selling at least $20,000 of agricultural products." The question is, should farm programs provide full-time incomes for underemployed farmers? Even farms producing $20,000 or more of farm products do not require full-time commitment from the farmer. Because families producing less than $20,000 annual sales receive all their disposable income from off-farm sources and about the same total incomes as nonfarm families, their inclusion in the farm population greatly distorts our view of economic conditions in the commercial agricultural sector.

"There is no longer any basis for arguing that farm incomes need to be supported."

Changing the definition of a farm would recognize that much of the human and physical capital investment in rural America is directed to "consuming" a rural way of life, rather than earning a competitive rate of return on that investment. Policymakers should recognize and gratefully accept the subsidization of food production that investors are willing to provide the American consumer, rather than trying to guarantee a competitive rate of return on their "farming" operations. If some such

families are judged to need welfare payments due to their low incomes, then their income maintenance will be achieved more efficiently through direct payments than through farm price-support programs. However, why should people get welfare when they have consciously chosen a way of life that has high psychic income at the expense of low money income? . . .

A Successful Farm Program

If direct payments to farmers are expected to correct the current farm crisis, they must focus on the source of the problem rather than the symptoms. Therefore, from an economic perspective, successful farm programs should have the following objectives:

• They should facilitate the movement of human and physical capital out of agriculture. The ongoing development and adoption of new agricultural technology will continue to require fewer people in the production process. Because of the widespread view of farming as a preferred way of life, however, there is a resistance among many farm families to move out of agriculture. Farm programs should help ease the exit problems of these producers, rather than creating artificially favorable conditions for them to stay in farming.

• They should remove artificial incentives to investment in agriculture. Farm programs that support commodity prices above market-clearing levels and tax policies that give preferential tax treatment to agricultural producers provide artificial incentives that are responsible for a sizable portion of agricultural overinvestment. The overinvestment problem involves land, as well as human and capital, resources. The Food and Agricultural Policy Research Institute (operated jointly by the University of Missouri and Iowa State University) estimates that 30,000,000 acres need to be withdrawn from production of the basic agricultural commodities in order to bring production in line with projected domestic and export demand over the next several years. . . .

• They should provide institutions and mechanisms that help farmers deal with the risk associated with uncertainties caused by weather and unstable world markcts. Price instability, often viewed as a primary problem in American agriculture, complicates the management of agricultural businesses. However, farm programs that artificially insulate farmers from that uncertainty provide the same artificial incentive to overinvestment as high price supports and special tax treatments. . . .

• They should replace current price-stabilization programs with expanded future markets. A 1983 Council for Agricultural Science and Technology report suggested that "a principal economic problem of food and agriculture is likely to be income instability." However, variability of supply and demand *per se* is not a serious problem in U.S. agriculture, and increased variability in U.S. farm income is not caused by "market failure." Rather, problems are created by the naive way in which agricultural market signals are interpreted by farmers and policymakers, who tend to treat price *increases* as a reflection of permanent expansion in markets for U.S. agricultural products, and price *declines* as caused by temporary weaknesses in demand that will soon disappear. This mentality, coupled with the distortion of market signals caused by price-support programs, tends to isolate U.S. agricultural producers from market reality.

If we had perfect information about the future there would be no need for government programs to help stabilize prices. However, even with perfect information and perfectly functioning markets, there would still be season-to-season variability in agricultural prices. Effective management of U.S. agricultural resources does not require perfectly stable farm prices and incomes—too much stability can be as costly as too much instability. . . .

Limiting Government's Role

The economic realities of today's agricultural sector are inconsistent with the assumptions and objectives of existing farm legislation. Consequently, price-support programs via voluntary supply-reduction schemes are increasingly expensive and frustrating to manage. Successful voluntary (subsidy-induced) supply-reduction programs require a continuing commitment to ever-higher levels of government expenditures.

"Why should people get welfare when they have consciously chosen a way of life that has high psychic income at the expense of low money income?"

For the past 50 years, it has been U.S. agricultural policy to develop programs that prevent agricultural markets from achieving equilibrium—and these programs have contributed to the problem of agricultural overinvestment. Future agricultural policy should facilitate a movement toward equilibrium in agricultural markets and develop programs that respond to the undesirable consequences of that adjustment. Successful farm programs must separate income-support and price-stabilization objectives; must meet the goal of income support by direct-income payments to qualified farmers; and must achieve price-stabilization objectives through the development of institutions that help producers and processors take a long-run view of market conditions.

To sum up, government programs have two major

roles in the effective operation of agricultural markets—first, the generation and distribution of information about current and future supply and demand; second, the development and operation of institutions that provide mechanisms for producers and processors to effectively manage the risk associated with agricultural production. Properly fulfilling these roles would result in much less direct government involvement in cash markets and would enable the U.S. agricultural sector to take advantage of its comparative advantage in world trade.

J. Bruce Bullock is chairman of the Department of Agricultural Economics at the University of Missouri in Columbia.

"Family farms are in keeping with the free enterprise system and offer the best assurance of abundant supplies of food."

viewpoint**122**

Family Farms Should Receive Government Support

Robert M. Frederick

Many have said that family farms will be and should be replaced by larger and larger farms that are organized on an industrial model of hired managers and workers. These same experts say that this challenge is necessary and inevitable. I disagree.

Let's be clear about the subject we are discussing. The family farm is somewhat similar to beauty—it's in the eyes of the beholder. If a family farm is understood to be a family-owned farm business (a business organizational structure), then nothing is seriously threatened as yet and the family farm is a viable economic unit. However, if a strict definition is applied (family ownership of land and other assets; family managerial control; family provision of farm labor; family livelihood derived from farming; sale of commodities in open markets), then family farms are a distinct minority and are undoubtedly beyond "saving."

All definitions are fraught with difficulties and are compounded by the regional diversity of U.S. agriculture and by the confusion over the use of the word "family" in "family farm." I would use the term "moderate-sized farms," rather than the definition distorting the term "family." To me, moderate is a range around the size necessary to achieve most economies of scale, fully utilize family labor, and produce an adequate family income. Under most such definitions, we are talking about roughly 500,000 farms, which represent about 20% of all farms and approximately 40% of all production.

Saving a Vital Community

The Grange [a national organization of rural families] has adopted the above approach in its definition of family farms. Family farms are in keeping with the free enterprise system and offer

the best assurance of abundant supplies of food and fiber at fair and reasonable prices to consumers than any other system of agriculture. According to the Grange definition, "a family farm is a business enterprise that is involved in the production of food, fiber and/or related products and services. It is owned and/or operated by members of a family who make the management and financial decisions and who supply most of the labor. It is of sufficient size to provide a living comparable to other segments of our society." If we can agree on what kind of moderate-sized farms we hope to be able to retain as the center of the structure of U.S. agriculture, we can then address the reasons why they should be retained and suggest some methods of directing public assistance to this sector of U.S. agriculture.

This sector of agriculture, regardless of definition, is in trouble and, in our judgment, must be the prime beneficiary of public assistance programs if rural communities are to survive. William D. Hefferman, professor of rural sociology at the University of Missouri, in *Can the Family Farm Survive?*, indicates that "the structure of agriculture has a bearing on the structure . . . the makeup and vitality . . . of the rural community."

Generally, moderate-sized farming fits best with traditional standards for a good community. A community of moderate-sized farms, regardless of organizational structure, rates highest, as a rule, in economic vitality; its citizens' involvement in community affairs; the number and strength of community institutions such as libraries, schools, and churches; and economic support for local agriculture input suppliers.

Planning for the Future

Marty Strange, director of the Center for Rural Affairs in Walthill, Neb., states four reasons why he believes moderate-sized farms should be saved:

First, there is almost universal agreement among

Robert M. Frederick, "Needed: A National Food and Agriculture Policy." Reprinted from USA TODAY MAGAZINE, July 1986. Copyright 1986 by the Society for the Advancement of Education.

economists who have studied the question of farm efficiency that when a farm is big enough to keep one or two people fully employed, it has reached full efficiency. You can't produce food any cheaper than on a farm that is human in scale.

Second, there is a greater tendency to appreciate the future and to conserve on farms where the owners hope to leave something for their children. In the family farming system, we have vested in the family the responsibility of stewardship of the land, which must sustain life for generations to come. That is a moral order that cannot be tolerated by the kind of farms that must maximize return on investment for owners who are not personally wrapped up in the land and its future. We might be able to require by regulation that corporate farms or investor-owned farms practice stewardship, but we have no right to expect that they will do so out of moral obligation. Corporations do nothing for the sake of virtue. They can live forever. They are alive, but they have no soul.

Third, the family farm is amazingly resilient. It rides the waves of trouble perhaps better than any enterprise in our economy. If the automobile industry had suffered the pain the farm economy has in the past three years, we would not only have widespread unemployment, but a shortage of cars. Not so with family farming. Because there are so many farms, each operated by an independent thinker who manages according to his or her own wits, all the farms rarely make the same decisions or suffer the same mistakes. Fortunately, a substantial core of farmers behaved conservatively in the 1970s, resisted the temptation to borrow against their equity in an inflated economy, did not expand on credit and they remain the anchor of the farm economy today.

Fourth, family farming brings with it certain democratic and community values—widespread ownership of economic resources, equality of opportunity, a belief in the dignity of work and the integrity of the individual, and a concern for the good of community. To the extent that family farming supports these values, it nourishes our social and political institutions; to the extent that it has abandoned these values, it undermines those institutions.

Ferdinand Hoefner, staff associate for Interfaith Action for Economic Justice, adds to the public debate over policy to save the moderate-sized farms:

> But beyond trying to neutralize the effects of public policy so that built-in artificial incentives and subsidies to bigness and absentee ownership are by and large removed, should we actively promote widespread farm ownership and the renewal of an agriculture based primarily on moderate-sized farms? Should support be given to beginning farmer assistance programs, cooperative purchasing, production and marketing arrangements, stricter estate and inheritance tax laws, progressive property taxes, continued basic farm family income protection programs and the like? I think so. Many economic and social values have been cited in support of this position. . . .

A National Blessing

The National Grange was established in 1867 during one of the most turbulent times in America's history. However, never in our 119-year history have American farmers been faced with social and economic problems of the magnitude they face today. What is most difficult to understand is why the most efficient producer of food and fiber the world has ever known should now be balanced on the thin edge of social and economic bankruptcy. The human and social values that are learned by people who are engaged in a commercial family farm enterprise have been overshadowed by economic forces that are beyond a farmer's control or comprehension. It is very easy to forget, and most people don't realize, that behind the abundance of food and fiber that blesses our country there stands an American farm family—a family which financially and socially sustains agriculture's infrastructure that encompasses an entire segment of our country called "rural America."

We would submit that the reason for Congressional committees and the Administration having labored as long as they did over provisions of the 1985 Farm Bill is because they refuse or are reluctant to come to grips with the questions posed by the National Grange: "What are the objectives of our food and agriculture policy?" and, more fundamentally, "What role do we expect agriculture to play in our society?" Is it in the national interest to maintain a system of commercial-sized, diversified family farm structures in American agriculture that will be able to sustain the economic/social structure of rural America? We firmly believe the answer is a resounding "yes"!

"Behind the abundance of food and fiber that blesses our country there stands an American farm family."

The two extreme farm program proposals that are pending before Congress are market-oriented towards a free market with decreasing support prices and phaseout of income supports; and strict mandatory production and marketing controls with high support prices and no income supports. Each would have the same devastating effect on the infrastructure of rural America. In the first case, human resources would be removed from agriculture, resulting in mega-farms being dependent upon world markets that are subject to actions of foreign governments. Those foreign governments have different objectives for their agricultural policy, leaving no assurance that our production could be absorbed. Such a domestic farm structure will lead to greater specialization, placing large percentages of our crop production at the risk of weather and other production hazards. More importantly, it would result in large, specialized agricultural enterprises that do not support local economies, leading to a demise of rural communities and the uprooting of a major segment of our social/economic society. The present depression in agriculture is more acute in areas that are dependent upon cash grain crops and that have lost diversification of income that results from a better mix of livestock-grain farm enterprises.

In the second proposal, strict mandatory production and marketing controls with high price support loans and no income supports will retain more human resources in agriculture, but would result in a shrinking of agriculture's productive base by as much as 50% in some crops in order to maintain the programs. Less farmland being farmed means fewer inputs being purchased from supporting industries and a corresponding loss of rural business and employment to sustain rural economies. In addition, the 70% of parity price supports would still leave thousands of small-to-medium-size family farmers unable to meet their variable out-of-pocket costs. The very farmers who need help the most would still be at a disadvantage when selling against the larger producers. After the program was in effect for a few years, our exports would be nil, further shrinking acreage under production and thus leading to further erosion of rural economies. Short-term solutions will bring about long-term problems that will stagnate U.S. agriculture.

Helping Farmers

Since 1978, the Grange has called for the targeting of farm program benefits to that class of farmers which is most in danger of being forced off the land. We submitted a plan to the Department of Agriculture (USDA) providing for variable deficiency payments which would be tied to the volume of production. It is but one method of targeting income supplement payments to that middle class of farmers who gross between $40,000 and $300,000 in farm sales. We are in agreement with provisions in proposed bills that place not only a limitation on payments, but also a cap on the amount one farmer can place under loan.

Perhaps it is time to recognize that supply control programs are just too indirect a route to take if our objective is to keep families farming land that they own or some day hope to buy. A direct income supplement with a means test appears to suggest itself as an appropriate device. It has been said that farm programs do not have a social responsibility. Granted, social objectives are not the primary driving force behind farm programs, but neither should farm programs or their administrators be oblivious to social consequences that farm programs and food and agricultural policy can cause. Therefore, the social implications of our over-all food and agricultural policy should be given strong consideration during the development of that policy.

Over the years, we have addressed farm policy in terms of the farm programs. In the 17 years that I have been in Washington, this is the fifth or sixth general farm bill in which I have participated, but

we have had a farm bill of some kind every year of those 17 years. We have moved from crisis to crisis in farm program development. The Grange, along with other farm organizations, has followed this trend and we have not addressed the issues that we feel should be addressed before we can develop farm programs. We do not have a clearly defined food and agriculture policy for the U.S.

The first AA [Agriculture Administration] Act and the following legislation was, I think, policy-oriented. It was done with a specific purpose in mind—a national policy. Since that time, I do not believe that we have addressed the broad, and more important, issue of developing a national food and agriculture policy. We further confuse the issue by using the term "farm programs" as a national food and agriculture policy. Farm programs are only a part of a policy and should be directed towards obtaining the objectives of a national food and agriculture policy.

Policy Objectives

In our judgment, if we define the objective we wish to achieve through our food and agriculture policy, the problems confronting agriculture's economy can then be addressed and more easily solved. We must answer the questions, "What are the objectives of our food and agriculture policy?" and "What role do we want productive agriculture to play in reaching our national objectives?"

"Family farming brings with it certain democratic and community values."

I can postulate a wide range of policy objectives, but the decision as to what objectives we, in fact, want to achieve is reserved for Congress and the Administration. For instance, is our objective to preserve and expand the U.S. share of the world markets for agricultural products or to expand the value of U.S. farm exports? Is our objective to improve the currently disastrous state of real net farm income or to reduce the U.S. Treasury's exposure on farm program costs? Is our objective to remedy the record U.S. balance of payments deficit or to continue to supply an abundance of low-cost food that only requires consumers to spend 15.9%, which includes that money spent away from home, of their disposable income for food? Is our objective to stabilize a badly deteriorated and still deteriorating economic situation throughout non-metropolitan America? Is it our objective to adopt a posture that will allow the debtor nations such as Brazil, Mexico, and Argentina to repay their loans to U.S. banks?

The list could go on and on, but every time I pose

these questions—and I posed them at every symposium and conference I attended in the last two years on the 1985 Farm Bill, I hear answers such as "yes" or "all of the above." The problem with such responses is that the right objectives listed are not mutually exclusive nor are they entirely compatible; therefore, someone must decide which of these objectives is most crucial.

The National Grange believes that the primary objective of a national food and agriculture policy should be to improve and stabilize a badly deteriorating economic base throughout non-metropolitan America. Many of the other objectives listed above will follow if profit is put back into family farming. Foreign policy and trade balance objectives of food and agriculture policy are in the public interest and the cost of these programs should not be borne only by the farm sector through lower prices or lower program benefits.

"The social implications of our over-all food and agricultural policy should be given strong consideration."

The Grange continues to support an agricultural policy that is "market-oriented." However, because forces outside the market impact upon the agricultural economy, we believe a national food and agriculture policy that provides agricultural producers with some measure of financial protection must remain a part of a future agricultural policy.

The policy question that must be answered by the American public is put well by Earl Heady of Iowa State University:

> American society needs to decide whether it wants a few large farms scattered alone over rural space or whether there are other values relating to rural space that are best maintained by an efficient set of moderate-sized family farm business enterprises. Unless public policy is changed soon, family farms, as most people know them, may disappear completely from agriculture.

The Grange believes that, in order to preserve the family farm business enterprise structure in American agriculture, we as a nation must answer Heady's question. We offer the following as a National Food and Agriculture Policy.

Establishing a Policy

Agriculture is the largest industry in the U.S. The agricultural system accounts for one-fifth of the gross national product and generates 23,000,000 jobs. Agriculture contributed $20,000,000,000 to the U.S. balance of payments in 1983, partially offsetting a large trade deficit in the non-agricultural sector. Thus, agriculture is economically important to the

entire nation. It is one of our most efficient and productive sectors. It is a sector that many feel has a distinct comparative advantage in production efficiency.

At present, approximately 112,000 farms—five percent of the total number of farms—produce just under 50% of the entire output of food and fiber originating in the continental U.S. These are operations that had annual sales of $200,000 or more in 1981. It is important to remember that these major producers are mostly family farms. The great bulk—somewhere around 95%—are individually owned and operated family farm businesses.

At the other end of the scale are the large majority of farms—1,700,000 of them comprising 71% of all economic units classified as farms by the USDA. These farms, with annual farm sales of less than $40,000, produce only 12.5% of total farm output. The great majority are part-time farmers who depend on off-farm income to meet their financial needs.

In the middle are the medium-sized traditional family farms. These make up a little less than one-fourth of all farms, some 580,000. They are predominantly family-owned and -operated, with the owner-operator engaged full time in farming pursuits. Sales run between $40,000 and $300,000 annually. They produce 38.5% of the output of U.S. agriculture.

The present structure of agriculture for the foreseeable future will remain much as it is now. The real question, therefore, is how can a program or programs be developed to meet the economic, social, and cultural conditions of these three diverse groups?

Social and Cultural Concerns

The small part-time producers will survive without the traditional Federal farm programs. However, a combination of state/Federal farm programs in the areas of research, education, health, medical science, roads, schools, etc. are important to the economic and social well-being of this group of nearly 2,000,000 American families.

The group of farmers at the top of the farm structure would do well without Federal farm programs. They can be best served by constructive trade and macroeconomic policies that are outside the realm of farm policy. They will benefit from government development efforts to stimulate the national economies of less-developed countries so they have the capability to purchase their increased food requirements. Export credit assistance, export market development, consistent international trade policy, stable and reasonably valued currency, and good infrastructure in the way of transportation and port facilities—all farmers would benefit from improvement in the above policies as the production of large farmers would move more into world markets, rather than being forced into the domestic market. Domestic policy to aid this group of large farmers would be in the area of research and a stable economic climate of growth. In addition, they would require some safety net of protection from vagaries of weather and actions of foreign governments that interrupt patterns of international trade.

Middle-Sized Family Farms

That leaves the middle group of 580,000 U.S. farmers who produce 38.5% of the output of U.S. agriculture and depend upon farm income to meet their financial needs. Perhaps the most difficult task will be to devise a program to deal with the needs of these middle-sized family farms. It is this group of farmers who should be the major recipients of the economic benefits of Federal farm programs. Programs should be developed that would assure these farms a return from the marketplace and from the farm programs that would enable the most efficient of them to continue to be viable contributors to our society.

We believe these farms are important to our national policy not only because they produce nearly 40% of our total food and fiber, but because they are a vital part of the social and cultural fabric of rural America as well.

Robert M. Frederick is legislative director of the National Grange, an organization of rural families that is based in Washington, DC.

Family Farms Should Not Receive Government Support

Clarence B. Carson

The plight of service station operators does not appear to ever have caught the public fancy. Not once in all my years as a diligent TV watcher can I recall having seen a special on the subject, or even a segment on the evening news about the disappearance of the family-operated service station. . . .

The Plight of the Farmer

By contrast—and what makes the above so remarkable—I have seen reams of material over the years dealing with "The Farm Problem." No presidential administration since that of Rutherford B. Hayes, at the latest, has managed to get by without some sort of "Farm Crisis." Every sort of scheme, crackpot or otherwise, to deal with the farm problem has had its advocates, and many a bill has made its way through state legislatures and Congress that was supposed to address the problems of farmers. For more than a hundred years now those who claimed to speak for farmers have proclaimed the responsibility of government to help farmers, and for nearly as long governments have been passing legislation of one sort or another that was supposed to do just that. Inflation—back in the days when everyone understood that meant an increase in the money supply—was once considered to be the panacea for farm problems. Then it was regulation of rail rates, government-sponsored loan programs to provide easy credit, government-sponsored cooperative storage and crop loan facilities, parity payments, subsidies, and so on. No history book worthy of the name is minus sections planted here and there through the accounts of the last hundred years detailing the plight of the farmers. And, according to spokesmen for farmers, the problem is apparently as urgent today as ever, what with declining foreign markets, drops in the prices of farm lands, and widespread farm foreclosures.

It is not my point, of course, that farmers have not had and do not have problems. As far back as my information goes, farmers have always had problems of one sort or another. They have ever been hampered in their enterprise by droughts, floods, plagues, disease, fat years when prices fell and lean years when prices might rise but they produced much less. Farmers have been going into debt ever since merchants, factors, or bankers could be found to extend credit, many of them going deeper in debt from year to year in the vain hope that bumper crops could be sold at high prices to rescue them. Anyone who doubts this should study the accounts of American farmers and planters in our own colonial history. There have been many changes in technology and farming methods over the years, but the sort of financial problems encountered by commercial farmers have not changed much.

My point, rather, is that it is not all that clear that farmers differ that much in having problems from the rest of us who are exposed to the exigencies of the market—which is to say all of us, to greater or lesser extent. Even government workers sometimes lose their jobs, and politicians do not always get re-elected. . . .

Farming Is a Business

The central point I wish to make, however, is that farming is a business. In this crucial respect, it is like a host of other businesses. It has been contrasted with operating a service station not because farming is essentially different but because a great deal of political attention and a large number of political programs have been enacted that were supposed to aid farmers. By contrast, very little notice has been paid to service stations, and except for an occasional piece of legislation dealing with the treatment of independents by suppliers, service

Clarence B. Carson, "Farming Is a Business," *The Freeman*, August 1986.

stations have rarely been singled out except for restrictive legislation. There are many other businesses for which there are no specific government aid programs: toymakers, for example, candy manufacturers, makers of cereals, and so on. Some businesses have been the objects of government programs which were supposed to aid them, of course, but none so massively, I think, nor over so long a period of time. Certainly businesses, in general, have not usually enjoyed public sympathy in this century; they have much more often been the subject of punitive regulation. Moreover, public opposition to and criticism of aiding other businesses has usually been vigorous.

"Theirs is in no sense more of a charitable undertaking than is operating a service station or providing hundreds of other goods or services."

Thus, it is important to emphasize that farming is a business. This is important for two reasons. First, it brings it into the correct framework for considering the appropriateness of providing aid. Second, it helps to cut away the alleged differences from other businesses. Farming for the market is a business. It is a business in that farmers use land, labor, and capital for the production of goods to be sold. Such farming is done in the hope and expectation of profit as are all other businesses. Farmers usually seek to use as little of the scarce elements of production as possible to produce the most of the goods that are wanted (as indicated by price in the market). They seek the widest market for their produce, and thus the highest prices available. Successful farmers keep careful accounts and plan their investments of time and capital so as to maximize their income. Theirs is in no sense more of a charitable undertaking than is operating a service station or providing hundreds of other goods or services. This is not to deny that there are public benefits from farming, but these do not appear to differ from those that attend hundreds of other enterprises.

Probably, a goodly amount of the public sympathy for farmers arises from memories that extend backward into an era when farming was often not so business-like as it has now become. The "family farm" may call up visions of small farms on which growing produce for the market was only an aspect of the undertaking. Such farms often kept a variety of animals—cows, horses, chickens, hogs, perhaps sheep or goats, geese, ducks—for family or farm use. Fruit trees would often provide fruit in season, and a variety of nuts might be produced. All sorts of crops might be grown, some for animal consumption, some for the family, and only one or a few for sale in the market. Such farms would frequently have surpluses of fruits and vegetables to be shared in season with neighbors and relatives. According to lore, and sometimes in fact, these farms were refuges for children who lived in cities and towns, to which they would be sent during summer vacation to spend some time on a farm with relatives, perhaps learning something of ancient virtues and values.

Today's Farm

Such farms have mainly gone with the wind, so to speak nowadays. Most farming for the market, whether on family farms or on company or corporation farms, is more or less highly specialized. Many farms today have no farm animals at all. The old-fashioned barn has often been dispensed with entirely. Vegetable gardens are probably no more common on large farms than they are in the suburbs. Machinery has long since replaced most animals for motive power on the farms, and the machinery has become much larger and usually much more highly specialized in function than it used to be. A family farm is distinguished from others, if at all, by the fact that most of the work is done by a single family and that the family lives on the land. Even when there is some diversity in the produce, it is still done on a commercial scale usually. In sum, farming for the market has become commercialized.

The great change in farming generally may have less bearing than might be supposed on government programs for farmers, except for its nostalgic role in promoting taxpayer support to "save the family farm." Actually, most government programs enacted over many years have been devised to affect farming for the market. Almost none of the programs has either sought or been devised to reward or restrict farm production for the family. True, some of the New Deal programs did try to encourage diversification on farms, but to the extent that they succeeded (by restricting the land planted to crops grown for the market), they usually resulted in driving people from the farms. Some loan programs, notably the Farmer's Home Administration, have enabled some people to buy houses on small plots of land, but these are rarely used for any significant farming.

In any case, most of the agitation for government programs and most of the actual programs have been aimed at altering the market in some way. One of the earliest interventions was an attempt to control freight rates and the prices charged for the storage of grain. These were supposed to help farmers who shipped their goods to market or stored them in the anticipation of higher prices. Currency inflation was aimed almost exclusively at raising farm prices or providing cheaper and easier credit. Parity programs were exclusively market oriented. The same could be said for assorted price support or subsidy programs. The huge government supported loan and insurance programs have been mainly used by farmers to purchase more land, insure commercial crops, or purchase farm machinery needed for large operations. In sum, government programs have usually been for those farming for the market, not for those mainly producing food for the family on family farms.

Farmers as Businessmen

To say that farming is a business is in no sense to downgrade its importance or to adversely criticize it. Nor do I mean to suggest that because farmers are businessmen, they are not entitled to a full measure of sympathy and understanding for the risks that they take and the benefit they provide for all of us. Farming is certainly a risky business, dependent as it is upon the elements, domestic prices, and changes in foreign markets.... Beyond these things they are subject to all sorts of exigencies, and work always with highly explosive materials.

"To say that farming is a business is in no sense to downgrade its importance or to adversely criticize it."

But to suggest that farmers deserve our understanding and appreciation should not be taken to mean that government should intervene either on their behalf or to restrict them. Farming is a business, and there is an abundance of evidence which suggests that not only is government intervention often harmful to consumers (that is, all of us) but also to those engaged in the particular businesses aimed at by the intervention. That farm programs over the years have benefited farmers is hardly self-evident. Undoubtedly, *some* farmers have benefited from some farm programs. There may even have been instances when farms generally have benefited, *temporarily*, from some particular programs. But that farmers generally have benefited in the long run from government programs could hardly be maintained (leaving out of consideration the cost to the rest of the population).

Farm programs are based on a faulty premise. They are generally premised on the notion that farmers engaged primarily in producing similar sorts of goods constitute a class with common interests. This might be so if they were producing almost exclusively for their own families. But to the extent that they are producing for the market, i.e., to the extent that farming is a business, their interests crucially diverge. A farmer is in competition with all other farmers producing the same type of goods when they enter the market.... Each farmer, so far as he is seeking a profit in the market, seeks to produce and sell as much as he can for the highest price at the lowest cost to himself.

The Rules of the Economy

Any government program premised on the notion that those farmers producing some one or combination of goods constitute a class with common interests is profoundly uneconomic. In order to work, it requires that each individual farmer act contrary to his own individual interest, that he regularly behave uneconomically.... If farmers were paid enough from government revenues to induce them to behave uneconomically as a rule, the result would be starvation and bankruptcy for citizens generally. That is, farmers would cease to produce those goods that are most wanted in sufficient supply to feed us. On the other hand, government intervention in the market to increase farm income by higher production tends to produce a glut of goods at the subsidized prices.

Price Manipulation

Most commonly, over the years, government intervention has been concerned with price manipulation: to raise the price of farm products, to raise the price, i.e., wages, of farm workers, to lower the price of shipping, storage, and farm machinery (by encouraging cooperatives), and to lower the price of money, i.e., interest. These attempts at price manipulation have sometimes been accompanied by restrictions on land planted to particular crops, on amounts farmers could sell of a crop in the market, on numbers of cows, for example, that a dairy farmer could have in production, and so on. Raising the prices of farm goods tends to encourage farmers to produce more and to draw others into growing those crops. Raising the price of farm labor tends to encourage the greater use of machinery, as does a reduction in interest rates. Restriction of acreage tends to shift farmers to efforts to produce more on less acreage, and so on. Government intervention tends to produce an ever normal "Farm Problem."

In fact, production for the market is a business. This is true whether the good produced is wheat or widgets. The rules of economy apply to farmers as much as they do to service station operators. We create the "Farm Problem" by lumping farmers together unnaturally and perpetuate it by government intervention. The solution lies in treating farming as a business and allowing those who can do it effectively to do so without interference.

Clarence B. Carson specializes in American intellectual history and is the author of several books.

"The longer we hesitate in embracing the free market, the worse it will be for all."

viewpoint 124

The Free Market Will Help Farmers

Dennis Bechara

On December 23, 1985, President Reagan signed into law the Food Security Act of 1985, commonly known as the "farm bill." This statute will affect the state of American agriculture for the next five years. During the past year, the precarious condition of the agricultural sector has been a hotly debated issue. Although the enactment of the 1985 farm bill is designed to confront and resolve the crisis, the unfortunate fact remains that the same failed tools which were utilized in the past will continue to be used in the future. It should not surprise us if more surpluses and low farm prices continue to plague the farm sector in the immediate future.

Why is our agricultural sector in such a precarious state? Is more government intervention the answer to the problem? . . .

The Present Crisis

Notwithstanding the massive subsidies farmers receive from the federal government, the farm economy is presently facing a severe crisis. Farm income has decreased by about a third during the past four years. In spite of this, the costs of the price support and market subsidies that form part of our national farm policy have ballooned to unprecedented levels. When the 1981 farm bill was enacted, it was expected to cost the taxpayers no more than $12 billion. Instead, the actual costs incurred amounted to over $60 billion. Similarly, in 1981, farm exports reached the unprecedented height of $44 billion, which represented approximately 60 per cent of the world's agricultural market. Our share of the market has subsequently declined to approximately 50 per cent and our exports were $32 billion in 1984.

The 1981 price support legislation enacted rigid and high price supports which only encouraged

other countries to further increase their production. Therefore, land values began to decline. Since the value of the collateral no longer supported more credit, financial institutions have reduced lending. Since 1981, around 200,000 farmers have gone out of business.

Because Federal price supports have been above market clearing levels, the government has acquired large stocks of surplus production. As a temporary solution, in 1983 the "Payment in Kind" (PIK) program was designed. Farmers who participated in the scheme were given comparable amounts of crops. Eighty-three million acres of cropland were idled, and the government surplus disappeared. But sales of fertilizer, machinery, feed and other products necessary for farming were reduced. Experts at Georgia State University estimated that the PIK program cost 200,000 jobs. This estimate does not include the actual amount of crops given away, worth approximately $10 billion.

Four Dangerous Mechanisms

The 1985 farm bill continues substantially the policies of the past. The outcome of these past policies has consistently been overproduction. In response to the surplus problem, Congress has established four mechanisms to combat surpluses. These are the acreage reduction programs, marketing agreements, voluntary land retirement, and import quotas. The 1985 bill continues this trend.

The acreage reduction program goes hand-in-hand with the price support mechanism. Essentially, if a farmer wishes to participate in the subsidy program, he or she is required to limit the acreage apportioned to the cultivation of the subsidized commodities.

Marketing orders represent another mechanism for dealing with the recurrent surplus problem. The marketing order scheme has its origins in the Capper-Volstead Act of 1922 which allowed the

Dennis Bechara, "The Continuing Plight of Agriculture," *The Freeman*, May 1986.

formation of agricultural cooperatives. This statute exempted agricultural cooperatives from the coverage of antitrust legislation. Even though the cooperatives were free to cartelize production, they were never able to effectively influence prices because not all producers agreed to join them. In other words, the forces of the market prevented the formation of monopolies. Therefore, further statutory intervention was required, which culminated in the Agricultural Marketing Agreement Act of 1937.

"If the price supports did not exist, farmers would guide production based upon market prices. When market prices are low, . . . farmers will act accordingly."

This statute authorized the Secretary of Agriculture to set up marketing orders for milk, vegetables, fruits and other minor products. Presently, there are 47 marketing orders in effect, covering a variety of crops worth around $5 billion a year. After a marketing order is adopted by the Secretary of Agriculture, a referendum of producers is held. If the order is ratified, it then comes into effect. The order may be amended from time to time by the Secretary, who usually follows the recommendation of producer administrative committees. Some of the marketing orders are not particularly important. For example, the market-support variety requires producers to contribute to an advertising fund. However, most of the marketing orders are designed to restrict supply in various ways. Some are concerned with setting quality standards. Others restrict the amount of products the farmer may bring to market, or determine how much fresh produce handlers may ship, or require producers to put part of their crop in storage until market conditions improve so as not to lower the market price. Any excess must be diverted for other uses, or simply left to waste.

Increasing Prices and Producing Waste

Predictably, the effect of marketing orders is to increase prices. In addition, resources are misallocated since supply-control orders, by raising prices, encourage more production of the commodity. This, in turn, produces more waste, since more commodities are then diverted to other uses or left to rot. It has been estimated, for example, that up to 30 per cent fewer acres would be needed to produce the amount of California and Arizona oranges which ultimately are marketed. Innovation is also reduced, since there is no incentive to reduce costs of production because a producer's sales are limited by the orders. An example of an innovation that has been frustrated is the development of a special shrink wrap that would allow lemons to be wrapped fresh for periods of about six months. It has also been estimated that 25 per cent of the lemon crop is wasted.

Voluntary land retirement has been a traditional method whose purpose has been to reduce agricultural production. In many instances, the additional purpose of fostering soil conservation has also been utilized as a means of limiting farm acreage. By the 1960s, 60 million acres had been removed from production. Ironically, the price support system and the disaster payment programs have encouraged farming in areas that have been subject to unusual environmental risks. For example, in the semi-arid climate of the Great Plains, ranchers may be tempted to cultivate some of the subsidized crops. After the prairie grasses are eliminated and a crop cultivated, the rancher may be required to set aside part of his land in order to receive the subsidies. This only exposes that soil to the dangers of erosion. The 1985 farm bill has recognized the deleterious effect of the price support system to certain erodible lands, and the eligibility of those lands in the subsidy program has been restricted.

Import quotas are the fourth method which has traditionally been used to combat surpluses. Sugar is one of the products that has consistently been protected from foreign competition. The domestic price of sugar is approximately four times the world price. Foreign-grown sugar may only be imported in limited quantities and from certain countries. The sugar quota allowed from foreign countries has decreased significantly over the past four years. In 1981 we imported 5 million tons of sugar, whereas by 1985 the amount was decreased to 1 million. This has foreign policy repercussions, since most sugar-producing countries are less-developed countries that urgently need foreign exchange to support their economies.

Disregarding Market Signals

In spite of these four methods of reducing surplus production, high price supports have consistently provided the incentive to engage in overproduction. If the price supports did not exist, farmers would guide production based upon market prices. When market prices are low, the signal communicated to producers is that production should be reduced, and farmers will act accordingly. With the present system, however, farmers can disregard the market signals and overproduce, confident that the government will guarantee a support price. The surplus production only succeeds in lowering market prices, which, in turn, becomes the political justification for keeping the price support system in effect.

One of the justifications for price supports and

marketing orders is that agriculture is a different type of industry. There are many aspects of the agricultural cycle that are beyond the control of farmers. Natural disasters, insect infestations and droughts are examples of the difficulties with which farmers have to contend. But there is a large segment of agriculture, over half of the sector, which operates without the benefit of price supports. Livestock, as well as many fruits and vegetables, have successfully operated without these supports.

The free market has the capability of protecting farmers against unforeseen price fluctuations through the trading of agricultural options. This system enables farmers to sell a commodity sometime in the future at a predetermined price. Since 1936, however, this system had not been allowed to operate in most of the major domestic commodities. But as a result of the enactment of the Futures Trading Act in 1982, the trading of agricultural options in the regulated commodities has been allowed. The first trading of these contracts began in October of 1984. It should be pointed out, however, that with the price support system in place, the prospects of these contracts are limited.

> *"The free market has the capability of protecting farmers against unforeseen price fluctuations."*

The current agricultural programs have inconsistent and conflicting effects. Some of the programs—like easy credit to buy and operate a farm, or research activities or irrigation projects—lower the costs of production. Other programs—some of the ones discussed in this article—tend to increase prices. Our legislated programs are encouraging overproduction, which has the unwanted effect of decreasing prices and reducing farm income. The surplus production which the federal government normally holds has been partially sold in the international markets. Foreign countries have increased their productive capacity, and this alternative no longer is viable in the long run. Our farm policy should not be based on sheer hope that some future event will take care of overproduction.

Embrace the Free Market

Circumstances have changed over the past fifty years. Farm income, as a percentage of the income generated in urban areas, has increased. The farm sector, on the average, earns about four-fifths of the earnings in the non-rural sector. Politics should be eliminated from our farm policy. It is not unknown for politicians to encourage the raising of price supports at strategically convenient times in order to gain votes. It is time we stop the present contradictory and negative farm programs. The longer we hesitate in embracing the free market, the worse it will be for all.

Dennis Bechara is an attorney and frequent contributor to The Freeman *magazine.*

"The Administration's so-called 'free market' farm plan [would set] in motion economic consequences felt far beyond the confines of the fenceposts."

viewpoint 125

The Free Market Will Not Help Farmers

Tom Harkin

Thomas Jefferson once wrote, "I trust the good sense of our country will see that its greatest prosperity depends on a due balance between agriculture, manufactures and commerce." Jefferson's maxim should serve today as a warning to an administration whose vaunted recovery has left the agricultural economy behind.

It is not altruism that must form the basis of our response to the farm crisis (though there is deep human suffering that can not be ignored), but a fundamental recognition of our national self-interest. It is my belief that only a dramatic change in farm policy, which acknowledges the value of widespread ownership of farmland and the need for a stable food supply, will be adequate to repair the damage of the past five years and rebuild our rural-based economy.

The farm crisis may have seemed to peak in the spring of 1985, when media attention to the problem reached a fevered pitch. Unfortunately, though public attention has waned since that time, the farm problem has not. In fact, it has worsened.

The fact that fewer farmers were foreclosed on in the spring of 1985 than originally predicted is attributable mainly to last-minute reprieves from local bankers. Many of those banks are now themselves nearly insolvent, so such generosity is not likely the next time around. Precious time was bought, but little else.

A recent study by Iowa State University shows that, if farm income continues to fall, 17% of the nation's farmland (25% in the Midwest) will soon end up on the auction block. An Iowa State economist termed the results of this study "mind-boggling" and observed, if current trends continue, "the financial problems will become so severe that it approaches a fairy tale—difficult to conceive."

These are not wealthy land speculators going out of business—most of those have already gone bankrupt. These are farmers with medium-sized family holdings, who are being squeezed out by five consecutive years of high interest rates, low farm prices, and mismanaged government programs.

Reagan's Damaging Policies

What we are witnessing is not just a massive displacement of family farmers, but a basic restructuring of American agriculture. To a certain extent, this has been going on for sometime, but the policies of the Reagan Administration have accelerated that process and brought us closer to the day of effective corporate control of all agricultural production. Ultimately, this will mean less competition, fewer choices for consumers, and higher food prices.

The ripple effect is felt all over the rural economy. Bank closings and small business bankruptcies are occurring at post-Depression record rates. In those cities with a large agricultural manufacturing base, tens of thousands of jobs have been lost.

The problem is not limited to the Midwest. A recent Wharton Econometrics study showed that, if the Administration's so-called "free market" farm plan were adopted, $50,000,000,000 in agricultural debt would be discharged, setting in motion economic consequences felt far beyond the confines of the fenceposts.

Wharton projects this would cost the American economy $74,000,000,000 in reduced business investment; 401,000 lost housing starts; 560,000 jobs; $35,700,000,000 in reduced personal income; and $96,700,000,000 in reduced GNP from 1985 through 1993. In addition, short-term interest rates would be increased by 2.75% and the Federal debt would increase $42,200,000,000 by 1993. Clearly, the problems in agriculture should be of concern to all

Tom Harkin, "America Needs a New Direction in Farm Policy." Reprinted from USA TODAY MAGAZINE, July 1986. Copyright 1986 by the Society for the Advancement of Education.

of us.

In developing a new farm program, we must understand that the fundamental problem in agriculture is overproduction. We do not have too many farmers (as Pres. Reagan would have us believe), but too much grain. We are drowning in a sea of surplus grain and [the 1986] harvest, the largest in history, will only exacerbate the problem. As long as surpluses stay high, and production exceeds demand, our farm economy will continue to decline. The Reagan Administration's so-called farm program would be laughable, if its effects were not so devastating.

Erroneous Assertions

Before moving on to my approach, let me first attempt to dispel some of the various assertions propagated to justify the Reagan Administration's approach to farm policy:

Farmers brought their problems upon themselves. Indeed, there were some wealthy farmers and outside land speculators who overextended themselves during the 1970s, betting that markets would continue to expand and land prices would continue to spiral far above their income-producing value. However, these farmers are far from typical, and most went bankrupt when the first crunch came in the late 1970s.

"We do not have too many farmers (as Pres. Reagan would have us believe), but too much grain."

Further, it should be remembered that it was Secretary of Agriculture Earl Butz who exhorted farmers to plant "fencerow to fencerow" during the last decade. Economists, bankers and credit officials, and other so-called "experts" all advised farmers to expand and borrow. Indeed, the farm credit system was rewarding its agents with year-end bonuses based solely on the number of loans made, regardless of whether they were well-collateralized. Farmers shouldn't be expected to take all the blame for the collapse of this house of cards.

Farm programs are too expensive. This is true today, but it has not always been so. The same programs that cost $3,000,000,000 per year under Pres. Jimmy Carter suddenly cost $12,000,000,000 per year under Reagan.

Sure, farm programs are going to be expensive when the floodgates of production are opened for two years (as Reagan did in 1981 and 1982) and then are slammed shut all at once with a massive acreage set-aside program (as Reagan did in 1983 with the Payment-In-Kind or PIK program. It should also be noted that 50% of total PIK benefits went to the

wealthiest five percent of the farmers—typical of Reagan's "give it to the big boys" philosophy.)

The solution to expensive farm programs is not to do away with them completely, but to manage them efficiently and with consistency of purpose in order to keep surpluses from building up.

The Role of Exports

What farmers need are more exports. Not necessarily. The export boom of the 1970s was a unique situation, caused largely by foreign droughts, particularly in the Soviet Union. Since that time, other countries—such as Argentina, Brazil, and China—have increased both their tillable acreage and their crop yields and now can directly compete with us for export markets. We can no longer count on export markets soaking up all our surplus grain.

Exports will continue to be important to farmers— by the year 2000, the U.S. Department of Agriculture predicts 50% of our total food production will go overseas—however, the real test of our export policy is not volume, but total revenues. Since 1981, agricultural export revenue has dropped by nearly 25%. What possible good does it do us to continue to export more if our farmers are getting less than the cost of production for producing those exports? Why does the Administration still insist on increasing export volume, even at the cost of lowering farm prices further?—perhaps to benefit the large grain trading companies. It is certainly not to benefit the farmers.

An Alternative to Reagan's Approach

There is, in fact, an alternative to the Reagan approach to farm policy which would substantially and immediately increase farm income while greatly reducing the costs to the Federal treasury. It is the "populist" idea of letting farmers determine by referendum—one farmer, one vote—whether they want to have a strong supply management program to boost prices through the same means used by every other industry in this country, matching supply with demand.

Along with several members of the House and Senate, I introduced a bill embodying these concepts, called "The Farm Policy Reform Act of 1985." This bill received support from a broad coalition of farm, labor, church, and banking organizations. It was written, in effect, by farmers themselves who participated in grassroots meetings held all over the country.

Here's how it would work: One referendum would be held to include the producers of all major commodities (wheat, corn, soybeans, etc.). If the referendum passed, every farmer would be required to set aside 15% of his tillable crop acres. If greater set-asides were needed for certain commodities, a progressive formula would be used to retire acreage from those producers whose gross income exceeded

$200,000. The bill also provides for a 30,000,000-acre conservation reserve and strong sodbuster provisions, to halt the tillage of the most highly erodible cropland.

Restricted supply would raise market prices above government support levels, eliminating the need for the bulk of Federal payments to farmers. Rather than the Administration's "production-only" program, this is the real "market-oriented" approach because here the farmer would get his income from the marketplace and not from government payments.

US and the World Market

As always, any dramatic change from the *status quo* is accompanied by strong objections. The argument is made that we will have to forfeit the export market or erect barriers against imports. In refutation of this smokescreen argument, my earlier points about exports still apply, but I would also point out two additional facts:

First, the U.S. supplies 60% of the feed grains and nearly 40% of the wheat in the world market. A recent statement by the Australian Wheat Board expressed the view that "because the USA is the world's largest exporter of wheat as well as being the world's residual supplier, the USA automatically sets the world base price for wheat."

Second, the U.S. is the only nation in the world that sells its grain in the international market through private grain companies. Every other country in the world—both capitalist and socialist—uses a governmental or quasi-governmental grain board to set the price at which that government will sell grain.

"The solution to expensive farm programs is not to do away with them completely, but to manage them efficiently."

Since the U.S. is the major world supplier, we set the price and other countries use their grain boards to peg their prices just below ours. If our prices are high, theirs are high, and vice versa. Regardless, our share of the total export market will not be dramatically affected.

It works like this: Suppose our market price of corn is $2.00 per bushel and the Soviet Union wants to buy 10,000,000 tons of corn. The Argentine Grain Board has 2,000,000 tons of corn to sell in the international market, so they approach the Soviet Union and offer those 2,000,000 tons at $1.95 per bushel. If the Soviet Union feels that it is not a good enough deal and balks, the Argentine Grain Board can keep coming down until they clear out their surplus. Therefore, the Soviet Union would buy

Argentina's 2,000,000 tons and the remaining 8,000,000 from the U.S.

If, however, the price of corn in the U.S. is $3.50 per bushel, will the Argentine Grain Board offer to sell 2,000,000 tons at $1.95 per bushel? Absolutely not—the Argentines will offer to sell their corn for $3.45 or $3.40 per bushel.

Raising the Price of Grain

So, in fact, if we raise the price of our grain, countries all over the world will do likewise. Why? Because it will be in their economic best interest to do so, especially Third World nations which rely upon the export earnings of their agricultural products to pay for their foreign debts.

The U.S. would benefit, since higher commodity prices would go a long way toward making Third World countries more self-sufficient in food, which can only improve world peace and order. With an increased standard of living, the Third World will become a better market, not just for our raw goods, but for our "value-added" and manufactured products.

There is no reward for flooding the world with cheap, surplus grain, either for us or for Third World countries who need to increase their standard of living. Once again, our goal should be to maximize export earnings, not just volume.

Of course, we can not turn our backs on the worldwide problem of hunger. That is why I have also proposed strengthening and expanding the P.L. 480 Food for Peace program, as well as domestic food assistance programs, to feed the hungry here and abroad.

Would higher farm prices increase domestic prices? Only slightly. For example, a $1.00 loaf of wheat bread contains only three to four cents worth of wheat. To increase the income of the family farmer 30% would mean about a penny increase on that loaf of bread.

As it is, Americans pay the lowest proportion of their income for food in the world. John F. Kennedy correctly saw the delicate balance that must be struck when he said, "It must be our purpose to see that farm products return a fair income because they are fairly priced. No farm program should exploit the consumer. But neither can it subsidize the consumer at the cost of subnormal incomes to the farmer."

A New Policy Needed

As of this writing, passage of such a far-reaching reform of farm policy—in light of staunch Administration opposition—does not appear likely. Where we have not succeeded legislatively, my hope is that we have begun to shift the debate and to show that there are, in fact, viable ways to help the farmer, if that is indeed our goal.

A continuation of current farm policies, though

better than the Reagan approach of abandoning the farmer to the "free market," will not be enough to avert further deterioration in the agricultural economy. Even if government support prices are frozen at current levels, farm income will continue to drop.

So, we will be back. Action deferred now will only be more urgently demanded in the coming years. We need only to look down the road a few years to see the grave social and economic costs that await us if nothing is done:

• The family farm system of agriculture will have disappeared, taking with it the rural communities it once supported.

• Our soil be depleted by erosion and our water polluted through the indiscriminate use of chemicals by huge farm operations.

• The Third World, much of it locked into unrepayable debt, will find it nearly impossible to earn enough income to feed its own people.

To ignore these consequences of the farm crisis is to put our nation in peril. What is out of balance must be set aright. The time has come for a new direction in American agricultural policy.

Tom Harkin, a Democratic senator from Iowa and a member of the congressional Agriculture Committee, has been a leading proponent of farm policy reform.

bibliography

The following bibliography of books, periodicals, and pamphlets is divided into chapter topics for the reader's convenience. The topics are in the same order as in the body of this *Opposing Viewpoints SOURCES.*

The World Debt Crisis

Alan N. Alpern — "Making Life Easier for Debtor Nations," *The New York Times,* February 7, 1987.

David O. Beim — "Must We Torpedo Our Banks?" *The New York Times,* May 4, 1987.

Benjamin J. Cohen — "Third World Debt (Cont.)," *The New York Times,* March 5, 1987.

Wayne Curtis — "Here Comes the Repo Man," *The Nation,* May 2, 1987.

The Economist — "Bidding To Compete," November 1, 1986.

Jaclyn Fierman — "John Reed's Bold Stroke," *Fortune,* June 22, 1987.

David D. Hale — "World's Largest Debtor," *Policy Review,* Fall 1986.

Bernard D. Nossiter — *The Global Struggle for More: Third World Conflicts with Rich Nations.* New York: Harper & Row, 1987.

Robert V. Roosa and Bruce K. MacLaury — "Deficits, Debt, and the World Economy," *The Brookings Review,* Fall 1986.

Frances Stewart — "Back to Keynesianism: Reforming the IMF," *World Policy Journal,* Summer 1987.

Howard M. Wachtel — *The Money Mandarins: The Making of a Supranational Economic Order.* New York: Pantheon, 1986.

William H. Wainwright — "Third World Debt: A Global Solution," *The New York Times,* April 9, 1987.

Trade

Henry J. Aaron et al. — *Economic Choices.* Washington, DC: The Brookings Institution, 1986.

Warren E. Buffett — "Here's a Radical Remedy for Our Trade Disease," *The Washington Post National Weekly Edition,* May 18, 1987.

Congressional Digest — "U.S. Foreign Trade Policy," June/July 1987.

Peter F. Drucker — "Beyond the Japanese Export Boom," *The Wall Street Journal,* January 6, 1987.

Martin Feldstein — "Correcting the Trade Deficit," *Foreign Affairs,* Spring 1987.

Richard A. Gephardt — "The New World of Foreign Trade," *The Washington Post,* April 20, 1987.

Phil Gramm — "America Needs More World Trade, Not Less," *The World & I,* May 1987.

John Heinz — "Why We Need Trade Legislation *Now,*" *The World & I,* May 1987.

J.R. Kearl — "Protectionism: The Myths," *The Freeman,* October 1986.

Carl Kester and Timothy A. Luehrman — "Why Dollar Bashing Doesn't Work," *Fortune,* October 27, 1986.

Robert Kuttner — "Guide to the GATT," *The New Republic,* September 15 and 22, 1986.

Jim Leach — "Protectionism: Good Fences Don't Make Good Neighbors," *Ripon Forum,* June 1987.

Anthony Lewis — "Coping with Japan," *The New York Times,* April 3, 1987.

Robert N. Mottice — "The U.S. Hasn't Lost Its Competitive Edge," *The Wall Street Journal,* April 3, 1987.

The New Republic — "Tradeamok," April 27, 1987.

The New Republic — "What Can America Sell?" May 25, 1987.

George R. Packard — "The Status and Power of Japan," *The National Interest,* Winter 1986/87.

Robert J. Samuelson — "Japan's Case of Malaise," *Newsweek,* May 4, 1987.

Male/Female Economics

Henry J. Aaron and Cameran M. Lougy — *The Comparable Worth Controversy.* Washington, DC: The Brookings Institution, 1986.

Steve Bartlett — "Should Congress Mandate Parental Leave for Employees?" *American Legion Magazine,* January 1987.

Barbara R. Bergmann — *The Economic Emergence of Women.* New York: Basic Books, 1986.

David Blankenhorn — "Why Paid Parental Leave Makes Sense," *The New York Times,* April 7, 1987.

John E. Buttarazzi — "Equal Pay for Unequal Work: The Fallacies of Comparable Worth," *Backgrounder,* September 29, 1986. Available from The Heritage Foundation, 214 Massachusetts Ave. NE, Washington, DC 20002.

Karen Diegmueller — "Laboring for Maternity Leave Policy," *Insight,* June 15, 1987.

Gertrude Ezorsky — "In Affirmative Action Numbers Count," *New Politics,* Summer 1987.

Ted Gest	"The Women Win—Again," *U.S. News & World Report*, April 6, 1987.	Lester C. Thurow	"Time To Retrain the American Farmer," *Technology Review*, May/June 1987.
James D. Gwartney	"Reasons Behind the Male-Female Pay Gap," *The Wall Street Journal*, March 20, 1987.	William Tucker	"Why Farm Subsidies Have Come a Cropper," *Reader's Digest*, January 1987.
Joyce Hollyday	"Women at Work," *Sojourners*, April 4, 1987.	Wendy L. Wall	"Farm Economy Slump May Be Near End," *The Wall Street Journal*, June 9, 1986.
Carol Kleiman	"Can Having a Baby Cost You Your Job?" *Family Circle*, August 1, 1986.		
Charlotte Low	"Caveats Reversed in Workplace Equality," *Insight*, April 27, 1987.		
Charlotte Low	"Time Off for Motherhood," *Insight*, April 27, 1987.		
National Review	"Tribal Justice," April 24, 1987.		
Eleanor Holmes Norton	"Step by Step, the Court Helps Affirmative Action," *The New York Times*, May 13, 1987.		
Clarence M. Pendleton Jr.	"Affirmative Action and Individual Freedom," *Lincoln Review*, Summer 1986.		
Aric Press	"A New Family Issue," *Newsweek*, January 26, 1987.		
Charles E. Rice	"The Legality of Equality," *The New American*, July 6, 1987.		
Daniel Seligman	"Brennanism," *Fortune*, April 27, 1987.		
The Wall Street Journal	"A Frontal Assault on Freedom," April 29, 1987.		
Amy Wilentz	"Garland's Bouquet," *Time*, January 26, 1987.		

Agriculture

Will D. Carpenter	"Bringing New Agricultural Technology to the Market," *Vital Speeches of the Day*, May 15, 1987.
Maurice J. Dingman	"Erosion in the Vineyard," *Sojourners*, October 1986.
Peter Downs	"Seeds of Discontent," *The Progressive*, July 1986.
Jerry Flint	"Some Problems Won't Go Away," *Forbes*, September 22, 1986.
Michael Fumento	"Some Dare Call Them Robber Barons," *National Review*, March 13, 1987.
Randy Geyerman	"Welfare for Farmers?" *Newsweek*, September 22, 1986.
Jay Habegger	"How the Fed Fooled the Farmers," *The Freeman*, May 1987.
James Lightfoot	"Farm Policy: 'Right or Wrong?'" *The Heritage Lectures*, July 24, 1986. Available from The Heritage Foundation, 214 Massachusetts Ave. NE, Washington, DC 20002.
Clifton Luttrell	"Government Crop Programs: High Costs and Few Gains," *USA Today*, July 1986.
John F. McManus	"Roots of the 'Farm Problem,'" *The New American*, May 5, 1986.
William K. Reilly	"Agriculture and the Environment," *Vital Speeches of the Day*, December 15, 1986.
Richard Rhodes	"A Yield Against the Odds," *Harper's Magazine*, April 1987.
Mark Ritchie and Kevin Ristau	"U.S. Farm Policy," *World Policy Journal*, Winter 1986/87.
Keith Schneider	"Farm Policy Is Broken, Ways To Fix It Are Many," *The New York Times*, September 18, 1986.
Hugh Sidey	"Bitter Harvest," *Time*, September 8, 1986.
Lee Smith	"How To Cut Farm Spending," *Fortune*, November 10, 1986.

index